A SOUL'S JOURNEY

Also, by G. C. De Pietro

Abandoned
The Story of Boys Forgotten

A SOUL'S JOURNEY

*The story of traveling through time
to find the truth*

G. C. DePietro

© G. C. DePietro, 2019

Published by Gloria DePietro

A CIP catalogue record for this book is available from the British Library.

ISBN 978-1-7343302-0-5 (Paperback)
ISBN 978-1-7343302-1-2 (ePub)
ISBN 978-1-7343302-2-9 (Mobi)

Book layout and cover design by Clare Brayshaw

Cover image © Raggedstonedesign | dreamstime.com

Prepared and printed by:

York Publishing Services Ltd
64 Hallfield Road
Layerthorpe
York YO31 7ZQ

Tel: 01904 431213

Website: www.yps-publishing.co.uk

This book is dedicated to Roger Woolger,
the teacher who opened the door for me to
understand the psychic relationship between the
here and now and the lifetimes that made me who I am.

CONTENTS

LIST OF FIGURES

CHARTS

ACKNOWLEDGEMENTS

Thank you to Valerie Legeay for her willingness to share her Clarissa story with me, which gave tremendous authenticity in the belief that soul groups do come back together to work out karmic complexes. And for her wonderful guidance through the years in processing so many of my own past lives.

Special thanks to Clare Brayshaw for her patience and expertise in taking my manuscript and transforming it into the book it is today.

Thanks to all those at York Publishing for their guidance and special efforts in making this book a reality.

INTRODUCTION

A Soul's Journey is an in-depth look at the learning experiences a soul acquires mentally and spiritually through the ages. It is difficult to separate the physical experience from the understanding of the soul, since the soul uses the body as its vehicle to manifest itself here on the earth plane. Everything our body experiences is recorded in the etheric field of our soul. Our appearance, mental attitude, health, and emotional state are all a culmination of lifetimes of working together physically and spiritually in order to grow and move forward.

You may ask, if this lifetime is a composite of all the other lifetimes, then why is there a need to know about the other lifetimes?

The reason it is important to know about our other lifetimes is that we have unfinished business from the past that we need to comprehend and heal. We all have unfinished business; otherwise, we wouldn't be here. It is here in this three-dimensional reality that we get to work these things out in order to graduate to a higher dimension. We can't move on until we have mastered three-dimensional reality. Once we get to the fourth dimension, there will be no need to incarnate any longer. In this third dimension, however, we are in a state of duality of cause and effect, creating karma as we go, which keeps us in the wheel of birth, death, and rebirth; all the emotions of fear, resentment, jealousy, and the like need to be transformed and cleansed in order to move forward.

What I discuss in this book is how easy it is to see the patterns and underlying scripts from the past that keep playing out in this lifetime looking for an explanation to a problem. If these issues aren't resolved in one lifetime, you will come back looking for a resolution. Your soul has a knowing, a consciousness, that directs you to the situations, people, and circumstances that play out the exact scenario that you need to correct.

Often, the lessons we need to learn are about compassion, forgiveness, tolerance, and love. It sounds so simple but look around. How many people do you see that are loving, caring, and nonjudgmental? Can you see anyone? Hopefully, the answer is yes, but I know as a group consciousness, we need to work very hard to be kinder and more loving to each other. If the emotions that we harbor, such as anger, hatred, bigotry, and jealousy, go unaddressed, they get lodged in the etheric field of our souls and cause illnesses. You can imagine how many events over many lifetimes have caused us to feel resentment and anxiety, which create phobias, compulsions, or even depression. Our soul will repeat the patterns until the need no longer exists, and then the patterns just fall away and stop happening.

An eye for an eye, a tooth for a tooth, we seem to be going around and around in a big circle. We need to take responsibility for our own actions and see our "shadow selves" in these situations. When we resonate with an event or situation – it is because we have an attachment to it. You can see yourself in it as a complex that you are trying to work out. Once you own your own shadow you can transmute it. You can look at yourself as a diamond in the rough that needs to be polished in order to shine.

This book suggests that by remembering past events, you can correct the wrongs that have been done. The events in your life are not random, even if they seem like they came out of left field. You were reincarnated for a reason you may not understand, but at the soul level, it makes perfect sense. As I was writing this book, analyzing the lifetimes that I could recall, I was surprised to find that some lifetimes seemed to balance out other lifetimes. For instance, if I lied in one life, then I was lied to in another. If I disrespected someone, it would come back to me, and I was disrespected. These were bitter lessons and hard for me to face, but it was necessary for me to understand in order to grow. All in all, there are 18 different stories that I can recall, many of which have contrasting learning experiences. Interestingly, these lifetimes all tie into some aspect of my present-day experience.

A trained past life regression therapist like myself can recognize the signs of what needs to be worked on during the initial interview. You don't have to believe in reincarnation for this process to work. During a past life regression session, you will be put into a relaxed state. Once you are relaxed, very little suggestion is needed for the memory to come up. Once it does, your story will surface, and you will be amazed at the amount of detailed information you can recall. As the story unfolds, your therapist will be able to direct you to all the unanswered questions you have that will untangle the hold this memory has on you. At that point, you can go on to your higher self to see what the big picture is in your overall growth, understanding how it fits into your karmic pattern. There, you can heal on many levels – the physical, mental, emotional, and spiritual planes.

As we enter this accelerated time of spiritual growth, it is imperative to let go of past life memories that keep you repeating old patterns. It is time to unlock the wheel of karma, of life, death, and rebirth. You can move on from this repetitive cycle by opening your heart and reclaiming who you really are – a perfect being of light and love. I have read many of the books on past life and reincarnation, most of which deal with case studies. This book is different in that the material presented is from my own past life memories. All the case studies in this book are my own, and in this way, I'm able to trace how these lifetimes have impacted the life I am presently living. Each story was carefully analyzed to see what the triggers were for me now and how I was able to trace these experiences back to the time and place where the complex originated. This is a fascinating study on how we reincarnate with certain soul groups to work out conflicts, reconnecting with loved ones in order to heal.

After years of studying, researching, and examining the evidence, I am confident in reporting to you what I know to be true, sound therapeutic evidence on the karmic cycle. This book is 15 years in the making, as I have carefully documented all these life stories in order to present them to you in a very candid and straight-forward manner. This work is a testimony to those who have had the determination to change the compulsive, repetitive patterns that keep them prisoners in their own bodies. I have seen transformations of so many who have overcome great adversity through this process. It does take courage to face your demons, but in the end, it is so invigorating and life-changing that it is all worthwhile. Thank you for taking the first step in reading this book.

CHAPTER ONE

THE WITHHELD TRUTH

Traversing the stars, flying around through different dimensions seemed normal to me as I lay in my hospital bed as a child. Being in the spirit realm was easy, so much easier than being sick, stuck in an infirmary. I didn't want to be in a physical body, I wanted to fly around and be free. After about five years, the doctors all gave up on me. That's when I miraculously improved. It took me a long time to figure out that I was supposed to be here; so much drama accompanied having a body, but after all the years of, being so sick I guess I decided to stay. Eventually, I did go home from the hospital, but I spent a good part of my childhood wondering why. Why was I here?

I knew all too well about the spirit realm; most people, however, had forgotten about their spirit or their soul. It is so easy to do; we get so caught up with the physical. After all, it takes a lot of work to clothe, feed oneself and provide shelter for. It pretty much takes up all our time. There is also a veil of secrecy around the knowledge of the spirit world. It appears we have forgotten how it is that we came here. There have been ancient teachings about the cycles of birth, death, and rebirth, but somehow these religious texts have been consigned to myth or some sort of divine intervention that has no place in today's world. I wondered how this distortion came about and why more people didn't remember being in a spirit form. If we go back to the earliest Christian writings, we find that the information has been manipulated into what the church wanted us to know. The fact is that Jesus himself taught about reincarnation and that the purpose for anyone to have a life at all was to remember where they came from. Thus, the work toward remembering brings us back to the source of all that is.

Jesus taught the true meaning of reincarnation. He taught it to St. Peter, and Peter taught it to St. Clement of Alexandria, who in turn taught it to Origen. Origen Adamantius (AD 185–254) is considered the father of the early Orthodox Church and Origen was one of the most influential figures in early Christian philosophy. Born in Alexandria, Egypt, Origen was placed at the crossroad of civilization. During that time, many influences from Buddhism and Hinduism circulated among the people of Alexandria, least of which was the belief in reincarnation, which became the foundation of Origen's thinking. Origen wrote in *Contra Celsum*, "The soul, which is immaterial and invisible in its nature, exists in no material place without having a body suited to the nature of that place; accordingly, it at one time puts off one body, which is necessary before, but which is no longer adequate in its changed state, and it exchanges it for a second" (Stemman 2005, 9).

Origen's belief in the preexistence of the soul and his belief that anyone could attain salvation was denounced by Demetrius, Bishop of Alexandria, who condemned Origen and declared him a heretic. Origen was tortured for his belief during the Decian persecution in AD 250 and died as a result of his injuries. Most of his writings were destroyed by Emperor Justinian I, who also denounced Origen. This is a great deception because much of the understanding of the belief in the soul's rebirth in the ancient world was lost as a result.

The apostle John may also point toward a belief in reincarnation. John 9:2–5, Jesus heals the blind man: As Jesus went along, he saw a man blind from birth; his disciples asked him, "Rabbi, who sinned, this man or his parents, that he was born blind?"

"Neither this man nor his parents sinned," said Jesus, "but this happened so that the works of God might be displayed in him."

This indicates to me that this man made a contract before he was born to be born blind so he would be available to manifest a miracle when he met Jesus. How else can one interpret that passage? God chose this man to be born with an affliction so that Jesus could display his healing power before men and inspire them to put their faith in him. (There are many references to generational blessings and curses in the Old Testament; e.g., Genesis 22:18 and Exodus 34:7).

> **18** And in thy seed shall all the nations of the earth be blessed; because thou hast obeyed my voice. (Genesis 22:18)

> **7** Keeping mercy for thousands, forgiving iniquity and transgression and sin, and that will by no means clear the guilty; visiting the iniquity of the fathers upon the children, and upon the children's children, unto the third and to the fourth generation. (Exodus 34:7)

It also begs the question of whether a man must sin to be born with an affliction. And what is meant by "sin"? Some reprehensible deed done in a previous lifetime. Jews define sin as breaking God's law as outlined in the first five books of the Old Testament, and Christians define it as disobedience to the teachings of the New Testament, which often overlap with those of the Old Testament, with the understanding that no one other than Jesus has ever lived a sinless life.

If you read Caroline Myss's book *Sacred Contracts: Awakening Your Divine Potential*, you will find that she explores the stories of many people who thought they knew what they wanted in life and had a plan in place to achieve a certain goal. Then, seemingly random events altered their course, bringing them to places they had never dreamed of. Myss explains how we are born to do certain things in our lives either due to karma from past life experiences or through grace by a divine source that has solicited us to do certain works here on earth. Life takes unexpected twists and turns only to bring us to the places we were meant to be. I don't believe anything is random. Who comes to mind is Mother Teresa. She was a woman with a mission; she was called to do the work she did, and if you ever read her biography you will find that there was an exact moment when she received the message to go to India and care for the afflicted. Don't we all wish it was that clear-cut? Most of us stumble around for decades before we figure out what it is that we came here to do.

I believe some people come here to learn life lessons, and others are here as teachers and guides. Thinking about the brave men and women who have altered the course of history, like Nelson Mandela or Martin Luther King Jr., it seems clear they came here with a distinct mission to complete.

How did humans reach this point in evolution when only about 25 percent of Christians today believe in reincarnation while Hindus and Buddhists believe reincarnation is normal, and the rest in the West think it is nonsense?

Let's look at the writings of Clement of Alexandria a disciple of Peter who suggested that Peter received secret teachings from Jesus. One of those teachings related to the concept of physical and spiritual rebirth. In 325 AD, bishops were called to the Turkish town of Nicea for the First Ecumenical Council. They sat down and discussed what the doctrine of the Catholic Church would be. They wrote the Nicean Creed, set holy days, and decided what scriptures would be kept in the Bible and which ones would be discarded. It's interesting to note that they aligned many holy days with existing pagan holidays to incorporate events that people were used to participating in. In that way the new church made its religion more palatable to converts.

But the idea of reincarnation was not a favorite with the new council. The bishops wanted the power to control the newly founded church. If they had left mention of being reborn to cleanse your soul in the church's literature, where would that have left them? If you didn't have to have an intermediary to get to God, why would you need the church? In addition, the language was difficult to translate, and so the ancient Greek and Hebrew scriptures may have been misinterpreted. The oldest, purest Bible is the Aleppo Codex, which is inaccessible. The versions available in the fourth century had already gone through changes from the original. One letter, one word, could alter the meaning of the text. I am not a scholar of ancient Biblical writing, but I imagine the Bible we have today is not the same as the original. Suffice it to say that the literature about reincarnation has either been lost or changed. By the Middle Ages, reincarnation was totally absent in Christian teachings.

Anna, the grandmother of Jesus, is one historic figure you don't hear much about. In fact, she is a remarkable person. She had to go through extensive teachings and trainings to cleanse her mind, heart, and body to prepare herself to bring Mary, the mother of Jesus, into the world. The book *Anna, Grandmother of Jesus*, written and channeled by Claire Heartsong, gives an amazing portrait of a holy, divine woman. Heartsong paints an intimate picture of Anna and the life and times of Jesus in a way that hasn't been done before. In this book there is an interesting passage called "The Story of Benjamin." Benjamin, a nephew to Jesus, was born with a club foot and often shook with palsy.

Lying down beside Benjamin one evening, Yeshua held his crippled hands as they continued to gaze rapturously into the starlit night. The moon had not yet risen. Gradually, Benjamin's breath began to soften and deepen. As his mind stilled, his Book of Life opened to his inner sight. He witnessed many lifetimes passing before him with all the errors for which he had not forgiven himself. He saw how he had shaken tight fists, had kicked and thrown himself at perceived enemies, cursing them to hell. He observed all manner of familiar patterns that he still repeated over and over, even though his intent was to be harmless and of service to his fellow beings. More than anything he began to understand why his soul had chosen to heal itself through a body that shook and walked with crippled limbs. (Heartsong, 2002, 220–221)

The passage goes on to say that Jesus gently placed his arms around Benjamin, laying his right hand over the boy's heart. "Silently, their consciousness joined as they traveled through the astral planes, gradually lifting burdens of guilt and shame. Benjamin's body no longer shook, and his limbs were no longer twisted" (Heartsong, 2002, 220–221).

In this passage it is clear that Benjamin was living a life of deformity because of the thoughts and actions he held from previous lives. In his present life, his soul could purify, and in his conscious mind he could forgive himself for his misguided thoughts and deeds of his past. It is interesting that each person's soul seems to have a predestined course. I know we have free will, and I suppose people can choose not to stay on their paths. But for those of us who are in touch with our heart's desires, we listen to the small voice in our hearts telling us to take a right turn instead of a left.

The situations we are born into seem to set the stage for what we have ultimately come here to do and learn. The soul groups we become part of are all part of the big picture of who we are meant to be with. The thought is that we meander through life's events, meet the people we are supposed to meet, have accidents that are meant to happen – that are not random – but happen to deliver us to a preordained destination. That structure intrigues me because it makes me believe that we do take some time planning before we enter a life to ensure we are in the right place at the right time. I have witnessed so many past life stories, and I'm always amazed by how the memory of a client is stirred when they recognize someone from a past life. They often say things like, "I know him" or "He was my brother in that life, but he is my son now." How about when we meet someone for the first time, and our blood runs cold, and we don't want to even be in the same room with the person? How do we explain that? Sometimes we find out in a past life regression that that very person was an informant in a past life who betrayed you.

Another common occurrence is when we meet someone, we feel like we have known forever, who seemed to have always been a friend. People in our close circle are part of our soul group; these are people we have reincarnated with many times.

The extraordinary story of Jesus is amazing on so many levels. If you look at it as Carolyn Myss does, Jesus's life was a contract that he accepted before his incarnation. That makes sense because he seemed to know he was chosen for a mission. He said many times, "I am here to do my Father's business." He knew he would die on a cross and then rise again in three days. His mission, according to the church, was to die for our sins, but I like to think that he died to prove to us that we don't really die, that we will all rise again. But the church doesn't focus on that, instead explaining that Jesus died for our sins, that there was a debt to pay for our original sin of partaking of the apple in the Garden of Eden. That is a manmade concept that puts the blame for Jesus's death on us mainly because we partook of the fruit of the tree of knowledge.

Why are we not allowed to have the knowledge? Is it because if we had the knowledge, we would not be able to be kept down, if we knew we had the ability to create our own reality we would be too powerful.

Instead, the Cabal (the controlling elite) destroyed our memory and told us we were disobedient and had to repent. Look at our history: it is crystal clear that we are debt slaves and have been from the beginning. Men have been programmed to fight their wars, to mine their gold and other raw materials; to build the pyramids and other civilizations, and we continue to provide manpower to work in factories and in little cubicles for the big industrial complex lifetime after lifetime. But if we remembered, if we had knowledge, would we continue to do it? It wasn't the sin of eating the apple, it was man's defiance, the desire to be on equal footing with the Gods. That is why we were punished. For over 500,000 years we have been enslaved, and I think it's time we woke up.

I believe that we die entrapped by our own sins, meaning negative thoughts and actions that we created in our own reality, time after time. This idea may seem radical to some, but if you think about it, isn't life experience the best teacher? If you mistreat someone, you should experience the same pain, so you know how it feels. If you steal, you should be stolen from; if you lie, you should be lied to. If you persecute someone, you should be persecuted in the same way: an eye for an eye, a tooth for a tooth. You reap what you sow. We create our own reality. But we can only break the cycle if we remember our thoughts and actions from our past lives.

That is how we learn. If someone lectures us on what not to do, do we listen to them? Only through fear do we listen. That is why the church invented hell. The thought of going to hell for all eternity would be enough to make people stay on the straight and narrow. But the church made sure that if we falter, God is forgiving, and he will absolve us of our sins. Of course, the church created and capitalized on that claim, and during the fourteenth and fifteenth centuries people could purchase forgiveness in the form of indulgences; combined of course with penance such as prayer and good works. Indulgences were said to give the faithful forgiveness for mortal sins and salvation from eternal damnation.

Indulgences brought tremendous revenue into the church which had a significant effect on the great Renaissance. The added revenue collected by the church made it possible for the church to acquire many great works of art. The church was able to hire the best artists the world had ever known; to create visual images so powerful it would influence the populace for generations to come. Whereby cementing their belief system into our psyche of hell and damnation, securing their power over us. The artists did what the church wanted them to do because it enabled them to have a life that was financially secure. It was visual propaganda in the image the church wanted to project. This scheme is exemplified in the sixteenth chapel by Michelangelo. If you look closely at the bottom section of the hell scene in the main hall, you will see that Michelangelo painted Pope Sixtus IV in hell as a sinner who would suffer for all eternity because of the relentless demands he put on Michelangelo to paint the scenes the way he wanted them to be done. At the same time, the Renaissance helped the church maintain control of the populace. Believing you could only be absolved of your sins through them took away people's power and kept them enslaved.

There is something to be said about the way people incarnate to correct transgressions. I think it's too easy to just pay for forgiveness. I don't think the soul learns a lesson on a deeper level that way. For example, take the life of a horrible slave master who performed hideous acts upon his innocent captives. Wouldn't it be just the key to understanding for him to come back as a slave? In this way, reincarnation teaches people that they could never get away with anything and would have to pay the ultimate price for everything they did. Live by the sword, die by the sword. At some point in the karmic cycle people would have to be brought to the place of awareness so they would knowingly right the wrong they had committed before. No wonder the church took those teachings out of the Bible; they are too empowering.

I never intended to become a past life regression practitioner. But life has a way of bringing you around to your life's purpose. As far back as I can remember, I wanted to be a painter. I begged my parents for lessons, and I dreamt about living in Paris and being among the great painters of the day. I read all the books about famous painters, and I thought the life of a painter was the most exciting life a person could possibly live. I was particularly drawn to the Paris Impressionists of the late 1800s.

The first chance I had to go to Paris was in 1977. I had already finished college and was disappointed in myself for not taking a semester abroad like so many of my classmates. I had earned a degree to teach art, but I didn't want to teach art; I wanted to live art. So, I saved my money and headed for Paris to paint for a year. I figured if nothing came of it and I found out that I wasn't good enough to make it as a painter, then I would go to Plan B. But of course, I had no idea what Plan B would be. As it turned out, I did well there. I painted for ten to twelve hours a day honing my skills, and in the process met and shared creative ideas with great painters from all over the world. I showed my work in galleries, sold almost everything I painted, won awards at juried competitions, and thought, *this is it; this is what I'll do for the rest of my life.*

The funny thing is that while I was in Paris I felt right at home. I seemed to know my way around, and it was interesting how different sounds and smells brought back memories. I remembered a life as a model for painters, another life as a seamstress, and yet another as a baker. Old cities have the power to do that, to bring you back to different times and places, like Rome, for example. I'm not a big fan of Rome. Oh, don't get me wrong; it's a beautiful place, and I love the people and history, but don't ask me to go into the catacombs. I will run the other way. I really knew Rome, too, especially near the Spanish Steps. That part of the city felt familiar to me, as if I had lived there before. The Keats–Shelley house at the base of the Spanish Steps was like going home. How can you explain knowing a place so well when you're visiting it for the first time?

Even though I had those experiences, I didn't give reincarnation much thought. I simply wondered why I had those memories if I hadn't lived there before. And if I had lived in Paris before, why was learning French so difficult?

A fundamental question that still plagues me is this: if we lived in different cultures with different belief structures before, why are we so intolerant of other cultures and customs now? For example, if in one life you were rich and, in another life, poor, why couldn't you see the importance of sharing? If you were once a slave in one life and a master in another, wouldn't you have mutual respect for other races and religions? How many times do we have to dance around an issue before we get it?

Why are we still fighting wars after many millennia of fighting wars? How many times do we have to die on the battlefield before we learn that no one ever really wins? I just think it's time to move on. If we are supposed to learn from our mistakes, why aren't we learning? Why do we still hate our neighbors and rape and pillage? How many more lifetimes do we have to live before we get it? I think part of the problem is that we don't remember what we did before.

David Wilcock, author of *The Ascension Mysteries,* says as individuals we have three 25,920-year cycles to get it right. After that, man must go to another density (a lesser density) on another planet or realm to finish working out their karma (Wilcock, 2016, 262).

Evidently, earth has an evolutionary process as well, and this planet is about to go into a fourth density plane, which is a much higher realm then the third density plane we are in now. That is why I believe it is so important to remember our past lives. I don't want to come back for another 25,920-year cycle. If this is the end of my third 25,920-year cycle, I've been reincarnating for some 75,000 years. I couldn't possibly remember that many lifetimes. But I do remember the important ones, the ones I need to review in order to move on.

External forces seem to keep a veil of amnesia over us. It's easier for the (controlling class) to keep us suppressed when we don't remember. What would happen if we all woke up and said, "I've had enough! I don't want to be manipulated any more. I want to be sovereign. I don't want to be beholden to my government, my church, my country, or even my station in life. I want to make up my mind about what I want and stop worrying if I have enough money to retire or whether I can pay my next utility bill." Is this a naive idea? Have I totally misread the signs of what it means to be human in the 21st century? Is it possible for each of us to be our own person?

There is a book called *The Ra Material, Law of One Book*. Some say this is the Ra of Egyptian times, but we have no verification of that. The book was channeled by Don Elkins, Carla Rueckert, and James Allen McCarty. The book states that reincarnation is one of the most important concepts to be grasped, for through it the universe functions and advances the evolution of mankind. This evolution is seen to be not only physical but also metaphysical, not only of the body but also of the spirit, and incarnations are seen in this system of philosophy to be opportunities for an individual to continue evolving through numerous and varied experiences (Ra, 1984, 17).

My understanding of this is that, first, the soul never dies and, second, the soul has an intelligence that is constantly seeking purification and unification with the source from which it came. At one time we were all one, but then we seemed to get lost and, worse, we seemed to forget where we came from. If I were the ultimate creator and I had this vast universe with all these beings, planets, stars, and galaxies, I would want them to experience all that there was to experience. But I would want them to remember their experiences so they could build upon them.

I'm sure the soul remembers all its incarnations, but the trick is for the mind and body to remember. That is the purpose of my investigation in this book. I have recorded dozens of my own lifetimes, and now I want to chart them to see how my journey has evolved so I can literally map my progress. I have gone to great lengths to uncover my past lives to figure out how it is that I wound up here. What I will attempt to do in this book is map out my journeys so we can all see how it is that the soul processes information and arrives at a given point in time to teach a specific lesson.

I think if people were to remember their past lives, things would be much different here on earth. If, for example, you were striving to be a millionaire, which seems to be a major goal for people today, would that goal change if you knew you had already achieved it in a previous lifetime? Would you be interested to know if you had been a pauper before and were afraid of being one again? That might make you go above and beyond to make sure you had enough. Or would you be happy with just enough?

I'm tired of not being taken seriously just because I'm not mega-rich. If no one had any money, then we could all relax and accept everyone for who they are, not for who they are trying to be. The quest for riches creates too much competition. Most lifetimes that I have experienced have been mundane. Meaning I've been a common person, a factory worker, a fisherman, a miner, or a farmer but these lives were extraordinary in a very real way, and the lessons learned have been profound.

I have come across an emperor or two, in my regression work but the most fascinating lifetime complexes are the ones about ordinary people who are simply trying to get by day to day. We all have been the good guy and the bad guy, the rich and the poor, the smart and the challenged. When I was working in residential treatment, I would often wonder why certain children were abandoned by their families or, worse yet, abused by them. I had to believe that such children had a vital lesson to learn about family, about love, and about resiliency. I found it hard to forgive parents who neglected their children or worse yet mistreated them. But I don't think the universe makes mistakes, so there had to be a good reason for their experience.

I have met many people who have come for regression work who are stuck in victim consciousness. That complex is easier to unravel after you discover where the client has come from. As their stories unfold, you can understand how they arrived at their present-day reality.

An emotion that is especially difficult to resolve is guilt. I remember a story of a man who was drunk one night, got into a fight, and went home with a bad attitude. He stumbled around until he knocked over a lantern, and the house caught on fire. Most of his family managed to get out of the house, but one of his daughters died in the fire. That poor man spent his lifetime trying to get over the guilt of what had happened that night. He had to pay the price for his action's life after life; he felt ashamed and angry mostly at himself and he couldn't forgive himself. So, when I see the nightly news and the horrific events of the day I know that there is a divine plan at work even though we can't see it from where we are, but each soul knows. At the end of the day when I process a story in a regression it often comes down to either forgiving yourself or forgiving someone else. And once you forgive others, you can move on to loving them and yourself.

Here is a story from *The Ra Material, Law of One* book about a boy who suffered from intense allergies. The boy's allergies were so bad he could hardly go outside. He seemed to be allergic to all living things; he couldn't play in the grass or smell the flowers, so he spent a good deal of time indoors. Under hypnosis he experienced, in detail, a long life in England. He had been a solitary man whose nature was to avoid contact with other humans. He had inherited a large estate and spent his life on it. His one pleasure was the extensive garden he maintained. In it his gardeners planted all manner of flowers, fruits, and vegetables.

After that past life had been discussed and the boy was still in a trance, the hypnotist asked the boy, as he often did, to contact his higher self. He had the boy ask his all-knowing self if the lesson of putting people first and other things second had been learned. The hypnotist then had the boy ask his higher self if the allergy could be removed because the lesson had been learned and the allergy was no longer necessary. The higher self said yes, it could. The hypnotist then carefully brought the boy out of his hypnotic state and walked over to the top of his piano on which was placed a magnolia blossom. The magnolia had dropped its pollen onto the polished surface of the piano. The hypnotist scraped the pollen into his hand, took it to the boy, and deliberately blew it into the boy's nose. "How could you do that?" the boy exclaimed. "You know how allergic I am." "Oh, really?" asked the hypnotist. "I don't see you sneezing." The boy remained cured of his allergies from that day onward (Ra, 1984, 18).

In my estimation this story needs further analysis. The English gentleman excluded everyone and was only interested in cultivating his plants. If I were regressing this person, I would want to know what happened to that young man that made him want to cloister himself. People need balance in their lives, but this man couldn't commune with his plants in this life and was forced to be with people. He had to learn to trust people again. I would have explored that circumstance further because the emotional aspect is so important to resolve. Shutting the world out is usually a response to some traumatic event, and if I was performing this regression, I would have wanted to know more. The physical ailment was healed, but I wonder if there wasn't an emotional layer that needed to be healed as well. When I do a regression, I focus on the emotional, physical, and spiritual layers so that every aspect of the life is processed and healed.

Nonetheless, this story is a wonderful example of how imprints from past lives can affect you today. I have always been interested in what happens to you after you die. That's because I was close to death so many times in my youth. That's a long story, but it's sufficient to say I received last rites three times. Being born prematurely at three pounds set me up for what was to follow. Many babies make it at that weight now, but in 1951 not so many did. I don't know if my soul was sure it wanted to stay around.

At about nine months I was diagnosed with nephrosis, a kidney disease that plagued me for years. It kept me in and out of hospitals through high fevers, pneumonia, pleurisy, peritonitis, and more. I know that seems dramatic, but I remember the priest being there and my mom saying her rosary. I created this painting to express what I remembered about the experience. Yet through it all I had the feeling there was a divine presence, thus I painted an angel at my side.

The doctors told my parents I probably wouldn't make it to adulthood. Isn't that a terrible thing to say? I don't know why people don't believe in miracles more. I was left with a feeling of, "Now what, since I have survived all of this, what am I expected to do? I must be here for some reason." That led me on a search to figure that out. What was I supposed to accomplish? Because of my near-death experiences, I have always known there is an unseen world, a world beyond the physical.

Figure 1 "Last Rites" oil on canvas by G.C. De Pietro

I can remember feeling my spirit fly around the hospital, going down the corridor and into other people's rooms and operating rooms, and just hanging around the ceiling looking down at my little body in the bed. It was a cool thing to do and I enjoyed it. I didn't want to be sick in that stinking bed so, I would fly around. The problem was that I didn't know how to control my flying experiences, and it would happen at the weirdest times.

That experience helped me when I worked in residential treatment because I could recognize their glazed looks as clients temporarily departed. When they came back, they would either cry or scream, which indicated they had been gone for more than just a few minutes. Being scared was all I needed to fly away. When the doctor came running in shouting, "Get the ice! Her temperature is climbing!" snap, I was out of there.

I think in the early days I was in a spiritual realm much of the time. I would console my mother, telling her that Jesus said I would be all right. I don't think a little girl of three years old would make up a thing like that. I wasn't afraid of the unseen world; I just didn't like all the drama of being in the hospital. I preferred to be in the celestial world where it was peaceful. The trick was to be able to go there when I wanted to go. But, of course, you can't function well in the real world when you are out of your body, that doesn't work, you can't be in two places at once, so you have to choose. It took me a long time to get my feet back on solid ground and to be present in a solid, physical world. The soul is such a flighty thing.

I remember reading a book by Ed Tick (a psychologist who worked with PTSD veterans) called *War and the Soul*. In the beginning Tick tells us about a man named Art, a machine gunner in Vietnam. Art said to Ed, "You can feel the connection between your body and your soul when it starts to break. It's like a thread that starts fraying. I concentrated so hard on trying to keep the thread from fraying. But I could feel it getting thinner and thinner" (Tick, 2005, 14,15).

One day Art was at his post on a hill when he remembered, "I was shooting and screaming for more ammo belts. I looked around, and I was the only one left. I could see my buddies running for the base. Yelling at me to run, there were too many

Viet Cong coming up the hill. I flew out of the foxhole like lightning. I could feel the bullets whizzing by me. I could hear their breathing. I knew I was a goner for sure. That's when it happened. I felt it, Doc. The cord snapped; my soul ran right out of my body. But it was way ahead of me. It was like it kept pulling me forward."

Then he goes on to say his soul never came back into his body. It was nearby, but his soul didn't feel safe enough to return. It hovered around him instead" (Tick, 2005, 14, 15).

That incident represents a severe case of PTSD. I know that is what happened to me. My soul would leave in times of terror only to come back when it was safe again. The thing is that parts of your soul can splinter off and get lost. That is what shamans are for. They are trained to retrieve the lost bits of our souls. I have been to several shamans over the years because I had such a hard time getting grounded. I have had several shamanic sessions in which lost parts of my soul were brought back and reintegrated with my body. I know when I am working with a particularly traumatizing story with a client that it was easy for the client's soul to get lost. I know to always check in, find the missing parts, and bring the missing part back before the end of the session.

Dissociation is only understood in the clinical, psychological world, through an analytical perspective, they get stuck in trying to rationalize what happens when you become traumatized. Psychologists know about the flight-or-fight response, they know about the physiology of what happens in the body during times of terror, but they don't talk about it or take it into consideration what happens to your soul. But the soul is what keeps us together; once we lose our soul, we are only a shell of a person. We miss out on so much because we are not fully present. We can have all the therapy in the world, but if we can't make our vessel safe enough for our soul to come back, it will stay away.

I worked with many traumatized kids as an art therapist, and I could tell in their drawings if they were dissociated. I had to educate my staff that yelling at them to complete a task or make their beds in the morning was only going to make them dissociate even more. Loud noises, yelling, and pushing is not the way to get kids to cooperate. When your psyche is elsewhere, you are not hearing what anyone is telling you.

Where does the soul go when it dissociates? That is a massive area of discussion. I think that your psyche finds a safe place to go in the spirit realm. Often that is with a departed relative or another protective entity, like a spirit guide that it feels safe with. Nature is also a safe place, under a rock, in a tree, a good hiding place can be found almost anywhere.

The way I learned to control my dissociation was through journey work or what you might call guided imagery. I can journey to the unseen world when I want to in a controlled way. I have taken my clients on guided imagery journeys through their imaginations and, to my surprise, they have been able to visit with their elders, with relatives, and with guides in the spiritual realms, something they did automatically when they dissociated, but now they learned to do in a controlled manner. Kids who dissociate, meaning who mentally depart from a threatening situation have the uncanny ability to meditate and journey through their imaginations better than anyone else can. It is the gift they learned while they dissociated. All they have to do is learn how to control it and to create a safe place where their soul can reside.

It's not surprising that it was exhilarating for me to finally meet Dr. Roger Woolger Ph.D. the Jungian analyst who taught me about past life regression. The psyche doesn't differentiate between various times, so what happened 200 years ago might as well be yesterday. That is why, when you enter a past life story, you can reenter the story and reclaim what was lost, correct what was not said, or forgive someone you fought with. The etheric realm of the soul is timeless and limitless. What you focus on in that moment is what your psyche believes to be true. Furthermore, only the stories that you need to revisit for your own personal growth in the current time and place will present themselves.

What is amazing to me is how much detail a past life story can include. You can acquire so much knowledge about history when you look back. Your soul knows what you need to revisit. Some lifetimes end abruptly without a goodbye or any time to adjust to the fact that you're in the spirit world. That is why you need to go back and process what happened to you. At the end of the day, all we really have is our stories, and I will share my stories with you about the places my soul has been.

CHAPTER TWO

TWIST OF FATE

I had been working as an art therapist with emotionally challenged children for several years. I worked with one boy who was about 14 years of age. He was placed in our facility while his mother finished her rehabilitation in a drug program. This young man was very hopeful that this time the rehab would work. His mother had been down this road many times but had failed to fully recover and would relapse. After she was discharged, she was supposed to come and visit with him. She didn't show up. It wasn't until months later that she surfaced after having gone missing. He knew that she had fallen once again. She finally showed up, obviously having been out in the street using again. This poor boy came to me after their visit had ended. He was screaming and crying, throwing things around my studio, and basically, he was inconsolable. He wanted to go home and be with his family again. He was the oldest sibling and felt responsible for the younger ones. He cried to me, "Why? Why did I have to be born to this crackhead? What have I done to deserve this life? Why couldn't I have been born to someone else?"

I was stunned, to be honest. I didn't have an answer for him. All I could do was offer support in his time of need. I did say to him that perhaps there was some lesson in all of this that he needed to learn.

That is when I asked myself, why does this boy have to go through this experience? He seemed to be such a good kid. All he wanted was to have his family back together again and for his mother to be there for them.

I decided I needed to find the answer. I wanted to know why terrible things happen to innocent children. Then I found Dr. Roger Woolger, Ph.D. He was teaching a retreat on past life regression, and I thought he might have some answers for me.

I attended the weeklong retreat in the Catskill Mountains with about ten other people from various walks of life, all interested in finding out about their past lives not for entertainment, but for clarity and healing. Some had recurring nightmares that wouldn't go away. Some had been in therapy with little results, attempting to heal from trauma, phobias, and other disturbances.

I just wanted to know whether one must pay for past actions, to explain the life of this young boy. What could he have done to deserve such a hard life now?

In the opening discussion, I learned that we do, in fact, have a lot of unfinished business from other lifetimes. That we come back time and again to work things out and correct the horrible things that have been done to us, and even some of the terrible things we have done to others. Not to even the score, but to heal from the scars of the past.

Dr. Woolger was very adept at teaching the form of therapy that he had developed, called Deep Memory Process® or DMP®. He explained that the body remembers everything and that the soul has a memory as well. Most of this information was stored in the cellular memory of the body and in the unconscious mind. What Roger asked us to do for our first introduction was relax and imagine that we were lifting off the ground and circling around the globe.

Eventually, we would come to a place that seemed to stand out to us, a place that held some interest. We were to find our way back to this place that was in a different time from our own. Our impressions of this place were to come back with us and we were to draw or write about our experience.

Mind you, this exercise didn't take more than 15 or 20 minutes, but the amount of information I gained was astounding. I recorded it in this drawing.

The caption reads, "I have to get out of here."

Figure 2: Drawing of the Russian Girl by G. C. De Pietro

The drawing shows St. Petersburg Square in Russia. I am the girl in the middle of the chaos. Cannons were firing, horses were galloping, troops were marching through the square, and people were running in all directions. It was total chaos.

Natasha, St. Petersburg, Russia, February 1917

I was immediately drawn to the square in St. Petersburg, Russia. I was able to draw the buildings there; I also saw horses and soldiers, cannons, and people running every which way. One girl stood in the middle of all of this. I was then instructed to add a phrase: if the young woman were talking, what would she say? What came to me was "I have to get out of here." This was the entry point into a life and time that I had no prior recollection of, but which seemed to resonate on many levels with the life I was presently living.

We split up into pairs, taking turns to regress each other. The goal was to regain our memories from our past lives. I was asked to repeat the phrase, "I have to get out of here." As the feeling began to mount, I could see the girl standing in the square. The regression began in the middle of all this chaos, which was really the end of the story, so we had to go back to the beginning. It became evident that I, the young woman, had died in the square. We slowed down the scene, and I was asked to return to the last significant moment before I arrived at the square. What I saw was like a basement apartment and I was with my mother and father. My name was Natasha. My mother was cooking something and preparing bundles to take on a trip. The atmosphere was tense, with talk of troops invading the city. No one knew exactly when the troops would arrive, but we felt an urgency to leave the city and go to our country home, where we would be safe. I announced that I would not leave the city without Boris, my boyfriend, so we planned a meeting location. I left to go find Boris, but when I got to the square, the troops had already arrived and there was so much noise and chaos that I couldn't find him.

I remember that it was very cold, and I wore a big wool coat with fur trim and a muff to keep my hands warm. I was approached by these soldiers, who asked me many questions. I told them that the people of the city were good, honest, hardworking people, that they had no right to invade this territory, and that the Tsar would hear of this and they would be punished. They laughed at me and started pushing me around, and I told them to leave me alone. They said that I was a foolish girl. The new regime was coming whether we liked it or not, and if we didn't do what we were told, there would be big trouble for all of us.

"You can't take away our Tsar!" I screamed.

"That's what you think, you stupid girl," they sneered. I spoke bravely to them in the face of danger, telling them that the history books would show the world that they were wrong and the story of the strong and wonderful people of St. Petersburg would be told. I tried to get away from them, but they tied my hands to a horse-drawn wagon as if to take me away somewhere. The horses were startled by the cannons and started to run. They dragged me a long way across the plaza. When the horses stopped running, my body was limp and bloody. The soldiers tossed me into the wagon. I don't remember anything after that. I felt completely disrespected by the soldiers, who had no regard for the life of one so young, so innocent, so pure. They cared not for her; she was merely a nuisance to be rid of. The girl was too outspoken, which got her into trouble, but she was right. The history books did show that the Bolsheviks took over. In the beginning, they were called the Russian Social Democratic Party, but soon after they came to power, they were renamed the Communist Party. It is interesting to note that I spent a large part of my childhood worrying about the Cold War between Russia and the US, which was not so far in the past I was born 34 years after this event took place. No wonder it was so present in my consciousness.

In the Bardo

The Bardo (spiritual realm) is what the Tibetans call a resting place or respite after a life ends, where one can go to review the events of the previous life. This is done by summoning others who were there in order to discuss what happened and find resolution. This is where the healing really takes place. Natasha called her lover and he came. "Boris, what happened to you?" she asked. "I was trying to find you." He came and told her that he had also tried to leave the city. On the way out, he saw my parents; they told him that she would not leave the city without him. He vowed to find her and bring her back to them, saying he would not leave until he found her. While looking for her, he was killed by the advancing troops.

Next, her parents were called in; they were so happy to be reunited. They had waited and waited, but when neither she nor Boris came back, they feared the worst because they had heard about the bloodbath that took place in the square that day. They admitted it was better that Boris and Natasha had been lost at the beginning of the troubled times because they passed years of hardship and starvation before succumbing to the harsh weather and meager living.

The soldiers who had killed the couple were called in next. They had no remorse for what they had done to the young Russian girl. She again told them that the story of the brave and good people would survive the massacre and that the world would know the truth. They had disrespected her, destroyed her hopes and dreams. How dare they ruin such a hopeful life? They said they had their orders and that the new regime did come; there was no way to stop it. But if it was any consolation, they had to live many lifetimes to undo what they had done in that life.

The village people were also called in. They all danced and sang together in the Bardo to reaffirm their worth and their traditions, and the small Russian family was reunited. The year was 1917.

After the workshop, I returned home and began to research the events that took place on that date in St. Petersburg, Russia. As it turned out, that was the year the Russian Revolution began. The Bolsheviks took over and deposed Tsar Nicholas, killing him and his entire family. It was the beginning of the Soviet Union, and indeed the history books have told the story of the atrocities that happened in Russia.

As for similarities to this lifetime, there are many. It is apparent that I have had to overcome feelings of being disrespected and feelings of worthlessness. Boris is now my husband Jack, who always thinks of himself as being bigger and taller. I tell him that that's because he was much taller when he was a Russian. I became obsessed with the feeling of having to find my boyfriend when I turned 25 years of age, which was about the age of our dear Natasha in the Russian story. I was filled with determination to find my true love and spent several years looking and wondering where he was. Now, I know a lot of girls become preoccupied at that age with finding "the one" – you know, the one you will be with for a lifetime. But this was different. I would stay up all night wondering where he was, where he could be, knowing he was out there somewhere. We finally met on a cold winter night in January. It's funny when I look back on that night; it was a snowy night, and I was dressed very similarly to the girl in my drawing. When my friends and I walked into the nightclub, I was wearing a wool coat with fur trim and a big furry hat. I saw this guy from across the room. When our eyes met, we both knew that we had finally found each other. But we did not stay together. When I made plans to study for a year in Europe, I didn't know then what I know now. This guy I had just met said, "You can't leave me. We just found each other" – an interesting choice of words. I have many letters in which Jack said he feared losing me or never seeing me again and begged me to come home so that we could finally be together.

He wrote to me every day while I was gone and eventually came to visit me in Paris. There is one photograph of Jack and me in a big square in Paris that reminds me of the story. The photo is black and white and eerily reminiscent of that Russian life. We got married in 1982 at the St. Moritz Hotel in New York City, which was located on Central Park West. The day of our wedding, hundreds of people marched along the park in an anti-nuclear war demonstration. I even marched the morning before the ceremony. Of course, back in those days, the main focus was our arms race with the Russians, which needed to be kept in check. I remember that the priest who performed our ceremony focused on an ancient text about a bride and groom who got married during a great battle and stood for freedom as they looked toward a future together. I thought it fit very nicely with the events of that day. But since the regression, I now know it meant so much more.

That night after the wedding reception was over, we were too excited to stay in our hotel, and we were starving. Since we had been so busy talking with everyone, we hadn't been able to eat much, so we went out on the town. We walked until we came to a little place near our hotel that was still serving. Guess where we wound up? The Russian Tea Room. This falls under the category of "You just can't make this stuff up." We dined on all the Russian delicacies. One last thing – since my husband is a singer-songwriter, he wrote a song for our wedding. The title of the song was "Thank God I Found You." Jack and I are still together, and we often talk about traveling to see the famous square in St. Petersburg, Russia. That should prove to be an interesting trip.

Another eerily familiar feeling was the day of September 11. I had just dropped off my kids at school on Forty-Eighth Street. I had no sooner got home when my husband called and told me to turn on the TV. I saw the plane strike the second tower. Panicked, I exclaimed, "You have to get the girls home safely!" The next day, we packed our bags and left for our country home. I was not going to get separated from my family and I wasn't going to be left in harm's way. If I had left St. Petersburg that day in 1917 instead of looking for Boris, I would not have been killed. It's such a strange coincidence.

So, what did I learn from that lifetime? For one thing, I learned that not even a revolution can stand in the way of true love. It seems that once the wheels are set in motion for a commitment or a vow, it will be accomplished even if it takes several lifetimes to complete. I have always been outspoken in politics and marched for causes I believe in. I have always known that war is not the answer. I have many Russian friends because the Tolstoy Foundation was in the town where Jack and I met and lived for the first four years of our marriage, then we moved to the section of the city that hosts the Russian consulate. I have embraced the Russian people. They are warm and very passionate. The Russian girl seemed to be well dressed, from a certain class of people in Russia who were out of favor during the revolution. This could have been one reason they singled her out of the crowd. It's also the reason there was a revolution, because of the disparity between the classes.

How does this register in my evolutionary process? I think the young girl standing up to the Bolsheviks was very brave. She believed in the sovereignty of her people, and even though she wanted to find her Boris, she wasn't going to let the Bolsheviks push her around. I think if one is going to die, it's best to die for something meaningful. History has proven her right. She died for what she believed in truth, freedom, and respect for a people who deserved better.

This was really quite an interesting story for my very first regression. I knew immediately that there were some definite similarities to that story and the events in my present life. To be honest, it took a long time to figure it all out, but this was just the first day of a long week of regressions. When we paired up, I would be regressed and then I would regress my partner. That was the method Dr. Woolger and his staff used to teach us how to do regressions. Sometimes they would do a demonstration along with practical knowledge of theory and science. It was a lot to take in and I definitely needed a week to process everything.

All in all, I did about six regressions: three I practiced with a partner, and three were done on me. The following regression was something I never would have thought of. I don't think the way regressions present themselves is necessarily in a linear fashion. The subconscious delivers whatever is needed at the moment and is most important for growth. The next regression took place in the mid-1700s in the Midwest.

Figure 3: Midwest Girl Drawing by G. C. De Pietro

My impression of the Midwest girl is that she may have been Norwegian in origin. I can't be sure about this, but the name Sorensen comes to mind perhaps Anna or Hannah. She was young around 13 or 14 years of age

Young Girl Settler, Midwest, (Late 1700s)

During the interview with the therapist, after a series of questions, a traumatic event from my adolescence came up. Why, I can't recall; it wasn't something I wanted to address. It was a night that my dad and I fought over why my mother left us. He yelled at me, perhaps because I was defending her, and said to me, "You don't know what you're talking about." He made me feel stupid. The phrase I went into the regression with was "What do I know? I don't know anything."

I began by breathing into these phrases: "I don't know anything" and "What do I know?"

The scene opened with a cabin being built somewhere in the plains in Middle America. It was in a big open field. I was helping my dad stack wood for the winter. My mother and baby brother were inside the cabin. My dad and I had just come in for some lunch when we heard the horses coming from outside. My mother cried out to me to run and save myself because she feared the worst. I saw my baby brother crying in the corner. He was young, about four or five years old. I looked into his big brown eyes and wanted to take him with me, but my mother wouldn't hear of it. "No, just go!" she insisted. "Save yourself." I ran out the back door and never looked back. I ran and ran until I couldn't run anymore. I decided to hide behind a huge rock.

I was breathing heavily, exhausted, and too afraid to come out from behind the massive boulder. I should have known that the Native Americans were excellent trackers and would have found me wherever I went. A native came up behind me. He grabbed me by the hair and didn't say anything. He raised his tomahawk and scalped me. I remember hearing him yelping, jumping up and down with joy that he had killed me. My dying thoughts were, "Why? Why did you do this to me?" I also remember thinking, "Why is he so happy to kill a sweet, innocent young girl? What did I do wrong?"

My spirit then traveled back to my cabin, looking for my family, because I wanted to be with them. I could see that they were all dead. The Native Americans had killed them all. I could still hear them celebrating this victory over the white man. My mother in that life was my sister Jane in this one. She was trying to save me. My brother looked like my nephew Dennis, and my dad in that life was my mother now. He didn't say much, just stood there and seemed to resign himself to his fate.

In the Bardo

I called the Native American up to the Bardo. He was still angry with me. I asked him why he was so angry with us since we hadn't done anything to them. Why couldn't they just leave us alone? He said we had taken the land without asking and it didn't belong to us. It was sacred Native American hunting ground and we had no right to be on it. I told him we didn't know that it was sacred land. "Isn't all the land sacred?" I asked. He said that it was his people's land, it was special to them, and my family had denigrated it. I said, "I thought God made the land for everyone to have and to use, not just the Natives." He explained that it made him angry when the white men thought the land was just there for the taking, with no regard for the people who came before them. I felt that the Natives should have been able to share their land, but he was adamant that this particular land was sacred to them and should have been respected. I told him that if they had come to us in the beginning and asked us not to build on their sacred land, we probably would have moved to an area that was open to settlers. This was about communicating and understanding each other. The Chief agreed that we could have worked something out, but so many treaties had previously been dishonored that he didn't trust the white man and no longer wanted to negotiate with him. This was an all-out war. So, we decided to bury the hatchet and smoke a peace pipe. All my family members were called in and the tribe of warriors were called back to sit together and smoke a peace pipe. The white people needed to learn respect and the Natives needed to learn to share. This we could all agree on. The warrior in that life was my father in this life. He seemed to still be carrying some anger about being disrespected, but he didn't respect women much. His favorite saying in this life was "Long hair, short brains," which gave a whole new meaning to being scalped, besides the double entendre implying that women were stupid.

In the Bardo, the Native took me to the river, cleansed the blood from my head, and reattached my scalp. The water was cleansing and healing.

The next day at the retreat, I took a shower and washed my hair. My hairline was different. I had always had a stubborn cowlick on the left side of my head that was now gone. The right side always seemed to bunch up in a clump of frizzy hair, but now it seemed more manageable and tamer. The part seemed different as well, with my hair simply relaxing and falling into place.

This story seemed so different from the last one. I was trying to figure out why it came up. Being made to feel stupid is not the best feeling in the world and being told you don't know anything is equally unsettling. In the story, apparently, I didn't know a lot of things. I didn't know we were on sacred land, just building a house with no care in the world. I also didn't know that Native Americans could track people anywhere. I thought I could hide from them, which was really ignorant. But my mom told me to run, and that is exactly what I did.

So, what did I learn from this lifetime? I seemed to be able to work things out in the Bardo with the Native American. We sat down and discussed what could have been done. The problem of the settlers was bigger than one family. It was disrespect for a culture and a people. I think that is what I said to the soldiers in the Russian story. How can you disrespect a sovereign people, the Russian people? The Native American was saying the same thing to me: how can you disrespect us and just come in here and take what doesn't belong to you? If you look at both stories side by side, one seems to reflect the other. I disrespected them, and then I was disrespected.

I feel that in both cases, communication was lacking. I can see that in most disputes, it is difficult to look at the bigger picture with a cool, calm, collected train of thought. I also think I have lived many lifetimes as a Native American and can sympathize with them, especially when I consider the way the Europeans came and took what didn't belong to them. The young girl learned a valuable lesson. Even though it wasn't her doing (she was following her parents' wishes), she paid the ultimate price for what they did. As far as I could tell, the theme of the week for me was respect – giving and receiving respect.

I couldn't imagine what else would be uncovered in the last round of regressions. I was reeling from the first two. I wondered whether my subconscious could be making these stories up. It seemed to me that maybe, based on all of my life experiences, my subconscious was pulling from all I knew to come up with these stories somehow. At the same time, I didn't know much about the Russian Revolution and had to look it up. It was only after my research that I was able to piece together the events that actually took place.

My experience has shown me that the subconscious mind will only deliver to your conscious mind the exact information you need at the moment of inquiry. If we were given all of the information from our past incarnations, I think we would be so overwhelmed that we would go insane. It would be way too much information to process and could be one of the reasons we come into this world with amnesia, unable to remember past lives. Also, we might be predisposed to certain people and situations if we knew about our previous involvement with them, thus altering the results of the encounter.

The information that comes up in any given regression is very profound and the exact antidote to the pertinent complex. Imagine the stories of rape, torture, abandonment, and desperation that are lurking in our collective memories. These are not easily assimilated. We know our history books are filled with these stories, which are at times surreal and may even seem preposterous. Yet, we know they did happen.

Take, for example, the "Trail of Tears." This tragedy really did happen. The United States government rounded up six tribes living in the Southeastern US and made them walk all the way to the Midwest, to reservations set aside for them to live on – thousands of miles to a place they didn't want to go, leaving all of their ancestral land behind. Over eight thousand people died along the way. They were disposed of without any remorse. Or how about Stalin? He was an interesting despot. He imprisoned over a million of his own people and executed approximately seven hundred thousand. Then, of course, we have the infamous Holocaust, in which more than six million Jews were annihilated, not to mention all the mentally ill, physically handicapped, and infirmed. Just about anyone deemed unfit for Hitler's perfect race was killed.

These are just a few of the stories in our collective unconscious. I have personally witnessed Holocaust stories, not only from those who were sent to the camps, but from the officers and townspeople who were part of the experiment. These people carry guilt, fear, helplessness, and emotions that will take lifetimes to repair. To think we have no connection to these events is naïve. We all carry impressions of these events and we need to heal as a people in order to be free. These are just a few of the horrific things we have done to each other, and they're hard to believe. But they are still going on. Just pick up the newspaper and read the headlines. We have Syria, North Korea, and natural disasters happening every day. I am at the point of not watching the evening news anymore because it's too much to take in.

I was nearing the end of the week and couldn't imagine what the last regression would be like, but I forged ahead, wanting to learn as much as I could. I have to say the group was very supportive and Dr. Woolger would often lighten the weight of the subject matter by making jokes: "The villagers are coming!" or "Oh, no! Not another hanging!" At times, it was very funny and helped us detach from the pain and misery of what had happened and focus on the repair work. This seemed to make it all worthwhile. I am always amazed at the stories that come up. I've learned about history and it is a validation when what I hear in a regression matches up with the actual events that occurred.

Debtor's Prison, (England, 1200)

This next regression really surprised me. I had no idea that I had lived in this time period, but after all I have said and done, it makes a lot of sense. The year was 1200 in England. The method used for the induction into this lifetime was pain that I was experiencing in the pelvic region. I kept thinking about the pain and was immediately transferred to a prison. It was cold, dark, and damp. I was standing with two men on either side of me who put me on a wheel with iron cuffs for my hands and feet. Since this appeared to be the place of my death, the regression practitioner asked me to go back to the last significant moment before I was sent to the prison.

This scene was in the English countryside. I was standing in front of a quaint little country cottage with a thatched roof, a thick wooden front door, shutters on the windows, and a couple of small rooms inside. I had a husband and three children. We also had chickens in a large chicken coop in the backyard. I was in the front yard when several soldiers came on horseback, sent by the king himself, John of England. They came demanding money for taxes. My husband was very vocal with them, saying, "Didn't we give you enough bloody money last time? Stop bothering us. We don't have any more to give you." He got into a tussle with one of them, and they took him into the backyard and hung him straightaway on a huge oak tree.

I grabbed the children and told them to run as fast as they could to their auntie's house. They knew the way. I told them they would be safe there. She would take care of them if anything happened to me. I told the oldest girl where I had the money hidden if she needed to come back for it, but to be careful and tell no one. Apparently, I did have some money saved, stashed away under the chicken coop. I was saving it for my oldest daughter, who had a terrible, crippling disease. I needed the money for a doctor in London that I was planning to take her to. I was determined to help my daughter, so I didn't want to hand over all of our hard-earned money to the king.

The guards turned their attention to me after the hanging, demanding that I hand over any money I had. They said that if I cooperated, they would let me go. I gave them what I had in the house, but I had no intention of digging up my savings. They were not satisfied. They yelled at me, saying, "We know you have more! Where is it?" They then tore through the house, looking through everything. I told them there was nothing more and they were wasting their time. They accused me of lying, then tied me up, threw me into the back of their wooden cart, and hauled me off to the debtor's prison.

Once there, they took me to a small room with a huge wheel in the middle. The prison was horrible, with people screaming and yelling. I couldn't believe what I was seeing and hearing, and I trembled with fear. They told me I would be tortured if I didn't tell them where the money was. I insisted there was no more. With that, they laid me on the wheel. It had iron cuffs that they put around my wrists and ankles. At this point, I told them I would never give my money to the likes of them and I didn't care what they did to me. They then lifted my skirt and jabbed a sword right up the middle of my body. I was screaming bloody murder, but no one could hear me above all the other screaming. I was in excruciating pain but determined not to give in to them. They stabbed me again and again, but I refused to give in. I was losing a lot of blood, but I was still conscious.

They then turned the wheel until I was upside down. The blood and guts turned around and fell into my lungs and throat, choking and suffocating me, drowning me in my own blood. I don't remember anything after that. They had literally turned my world upside down. The feeling I had during the regression was so disorienting that I felt like vomiting. I became so dizzy that I was actually sick to my stomach in real time.

I died on the wheel and never saw my children again. I was dizzy for days after that regression. I had no idea why this lifetime came up. Let's review the evidence and see what comparisons there are to my present lifetime. My husband in that lifetime was a man I knew in my mid-twenties. We dated for about a year and a half, and I thought he might have been the one, but he died suddenly at the age of 35. He died of a heart attack, and I have no idea if he was the same age in the story I just told, but it's interesting that he died so young. I remember a time while we were dating when I had a pelvic infection, oddly enough, and went to see the doctor. When I returned, he asked me, "What did those butchers do to you?" That was an odd choice of words, but truth be told, it could have been a deeply rooted subconscious thought.

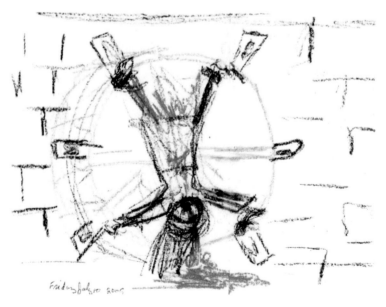

Figure 4: The Wheel, drawing by G. C. De Pietro

Also, he died suddenly and unexpectedly in the English lifetime and I didn't have time to mourn his passing because the soldiers took me to the prison however, I was able to mourn his passing in this life.

The young daughter in the story is my daughter today. When she was about twelve years old, she contracted Lyme disease, and I was beside myself to find a cure for her. It took several years to cure her, and by the time we found the right doctor she could barely walk on her own. I left no stone unturned to get her the help she needed. I did spend a lot of money on doctors, but I don't recall it interfering with my ability to pay my taxes, although I never seem to have enough money for taxes and it is a thorn in my side (Oops. No pun intended!). Today, one can work out a payment plan with the IRS – not so much with King John back in the 1200s. As for lying to the authorities, I am very careful to have my accountant follow the rules of engagement when it comes to the IRS. At the same time, I'm not afraid to look for deductions. I still feel that the government asks far too much and never seems to be satisfied. I can relate to George Harrison's song "Taxman."

In the Bardo

I had thought, back in the 1200s, that when I told the children to run to their auntie's house, she would take the hidden money to help my daughter by taking her to the doctor to get cured. As it turned out, in the Bardo I found out that because times were hard and my sister was suddenly asked to take in three more children, she had to use the money to feed them all. Thus, my girl in that day didn't get the treatment she needed from the doctor in London. She became a cripple and died young in that life. That could be the reason it was left unfinished and had to be revisited in this lifetime. I don't recall who the other two children were, but my sister in that lifetime is also my sister in this one.

I did some research and found a few torture devices from that time period that included a wheel. These were not exactly like the one I pictured, but that doesn't mean it didn't exist. I am left feeling that as a woman, I was attacked in a way that diminished my feminine power and the message was that I could not challenge the authorities and win. This theme will be seen again in other regressions in which my feminine power is kept in check.

As I think about that life, I realize there were several issues left unresolved: losing my husband, not taking care of my daughter's health, and lying to the authorities about not having the money when I did. I paid a huge price for that, but is it over? Is the stain still left on my soul? We will see if it's erased in subsequent lifetimes.

Figure 5: Catherine Wheel   *Figure 6: History of Medieval Torture Devices*

Here are two wheel-oriented torture devices found in the history books

Slave Boy in Ancient Times (fourth or fifth century)

Thinking about my deception, I went to a friend who could access the Akashic records, in which all is written for those who have the stomach to read the truth about themselves. I wanted to know whether the lesson about truth was ever addressed. The following is what transpired.

From the records, I learned that there was a gate that was closed to me because of a deceit, a falsehood I had told to a nobleman who wanted to purchase me, a young slave boy, and bring me to freedom. But I was so afraid of not being chosen to live with the nobleman's family that I lied about my own sister. I was jealous because I wanted him to choose me instead of her.

I told the master that she had stolen money from him and deceived him so he would find favor with me instead. When the master discovered that I had lied to him, he cast me aside and chose the girl for freedom. He told me that I would never be able to survive on my own, that I was doomed to grovel and beg, that I was unworthy. Not being chosen meant that I would spend the rest of my days as a beggar in servitude.

In my defense, I pleaded, "But Master, she would have sold me to the devil himself if she thought she could be free. Maybe she didn't steal money from you, but she would do anything to be free and so would I. What can I do to make it up to you? I admit I took the money and blamed her so that you would look upon me favorably and set me free. I admit what I did. She must also admit that she taunted me, saying she was prettier and more desirable than me, that I was second best and would never be chosen over her. So, I tried to tip the scales in my favor."

The master said, "I favored you more because I wanted a son, having lost my only son. I fooled myself into thinking you were beyond reproach. I was so disappointed in you when I heard that you lied to me, I became angry and despondent. Now I know you cannot live up to my expectations. And I curse you for it."

"Please don't shut me out!" I begged. "I have learned that the truth is the only thing that can truly set me free, and I want to prove to you that I can be trustworthy. I have been chained so long by my own deceit that I have been ashamed to ask you for forgiveness. I was blinded by my own longings and wants and lied for my own benefit. I would rather have your forgiveness than anything else in the world, more than money or freedom, if you could find it in your heart to accept me. I will work very hard to fight for the truth in all things and never lower myself again to tell an easy lie for personal gain. I will stand my ground and tell the truth if you will release me from this bondage."

The master said, "I did curse you, but I have not kept you in bondage; rather, your own guilt has kept you there. If you can forgive yourself for what you have done, you will regain your dignity and be able to stand up for what is righteous. I will not oppose you. You have learned a valuable lesson."

The angels came to cleanse the boy of his guilt and help restore his dignity. I asked the master, "Who are you?"

"I am your conscience," the master replied.

"I take responsibility for all my actions, past and present, and promise to move forward in truth. My mission is to tell the truth in all matters, to not be afraid to do so because it is only by telling the truth that one can be forgiven. I forgive myself for past transgressions and let go of any guilt still present, to honor and love myself as a true bearer of the light to the world." Said the slave boy.

This was an amazing lesson for a young boy to learn. I would think that the slave boy lived in the fourth or fifth century; not having done this regression for myself, I could only guess at the timeline. I also wonder if a soul has parallel lives living simultaneously in other realms. I ponder this because some of the lifetimes I did review seemed to carry the same themes as this story, overlapping each other.

Political Activist, (Scotland, 1920s)

The last regression, in the year 2008, is that of a political activist. This regression was done by Patricia Walsh, Practitioner/ Chief Trainer – Deep Memory Process ® and Dr. Woolger's longtime associate and workshop trainer; she recorded it for possible inclusion in promotional material. The thought that prompted this regression was "They never listen to me." The scene opened with a young man speaking in front of a crowd of people who were jeering and yelling at him. The young man realized the crowd was about to get hostile, so he retreated from the podium to a backstage area. There, he met a small group of supporters. They reviewed a map that suggested an escape route from the town to a place of refuge. This respite would give him the time he needed to regroup until a better time to come back and address his people. They ushered him out to a cart that took him to a hilltop shelter. This suggests the events took place in the mid-eighteenth century; I feel that it was in Scotland or some place with a lot of sheep and rolling hills.

At the hilltop retreat, the activist is greeted by men with guns. They show him to a room to wait. He is then asked to meet with a general, who comes to offer him a deal. They will pay him to leave the area so that a militia group can then come in and take over the area. He refuses. Shortly afterward, at nightfall, they see a large group of peasants coming up the hill with torches to take the activist. They are angry with him because they think he is getting in the way of their progress. They are part of a political group that wants to usher in the industrial revolution sweeping across major cities in their region, and they want to change the rural nature of the people's work environment.

This young man is fighting to keep the traditions of his people, trying to keep the development out, and they see him as a hindrance. He tells them that they have always worked the land and they should not give up their farms for industry. Even though his family consists of the wealthiest landowners in the area, they don't want to give up their land to factories. The activist doesn't trust these capitalists, who are telling his people they will give them good jobs. He only sees them enslaving the people in factories, giving them little in return.

The people are tired of working the land and they think this is an opportunity for change. Since they feel he is standing in their way, they want to get rid of him, so they come to the compound demanding he step down. They break down the door, take him out to the yard, and hang him. But before he dies, he says to them, "You don't understand what you are doing. You will regret this."

They don't listen to him, and instead silence him forever. This crystallizes the beginning phrase, "They never listen to me." This was the imprint left, and the feeling that was carried over into this lifetime.

In the Bardo

In the Bardo, the activist made peace with the villagers. They came to him and told him that they were given very little for their land, then the investors-built factories and offered them low paying jobs that they hated. They had lost their beautiful way of life. This validated his life, offering him some credit for the message he had brought them. In the Bardo, he was reunited with his family, who had never given up on their brave son. The general and his militia were not welcomed into the Bardo. They had to go back and make restitution for destroying the land.

Finally, a little chickadee came to the Bardo to offer this young man strength in a talisman as the bearer of truth. (This is funny because I forgot about this regression and chose the chickadee as my logo without remembering its meaning.) The song of the chickadee is sweet and appealing to those who hear it and are willing to listen. They know the song he sings is the song of truth.

In the workplace before I retired from doing art therapy is where I felt this truth the most. The administration didn't want to hear my ideas about expanding the art therapy department, which I developed and chaired. They totally ignored my efforts to recruit interns, which would have brought art therapy to many more children on the campus. Instead, they took a different route. I eventually left that job, seeing that there was no room for growth.

Then again, in this present life, I was involved with a grassroots organization that worked to keep the big box stores out of our rural area. I started a campaign to raise awareness of the local people by painting murals all over town that addressed the history of our area. The Hudson Valley, where I live, is full of interesting stories of people and events from the 1600s and 1700s, which were depicted in these scenes. It seemed to work, and to this day we have managed to preserve the country feel and keep the farms intact. I'm so happy the villagers agreed with me this time around.

This story of the political activist also echoes the story of the young girl who was scalped by the Native American. She felt that the white people didn't know what they were doing by settling on the Native American' sacred hunting ground. The phrase for that regression was "I don't know anything." This time, he did know what he was talking about; he had all the facts, but no one could hear him, no one wanted to hear him, because they wanted something different. And what about the Russian girl who stood up to the soldiers for what she believed in? She was caught in the middle of a political overthrow.

I am beginning to see a pattern of truth-telling, which seems to be a theme in many of my regressions. Could it be that there was a very dark shadow life in which the lie I told affected many people? We will see in this next past life story how truth and lies come home to roost. This young brave was naïve and fell for the biggest of lies. In this life, I feel that my soul learned the consequences of being lied to.

Native American Brave (Mid-1600s)

The phrase I used to enter into this regression after a lot of soul searching was "They don't want me." After I repeated it several times, the image I saw was of a young Native American boy about 12 or 13 years old. He was going on his first solo hunting expedition. This was his rite of passage into manhood. I could see him leaving his village. I was speaking in the third person, and Pat the group leader, came over to me and said, "Get into your body and tell me, boy, what are you feeling?"

I saw a bear's cave as I approached it, I rustled some leaves and the bear came out. He saw me and stood upright about seven or eight feet tall. To me he was huge, but because he stood up, I had a clear shot at his heart with my arrow. I shot him, but he kept coming after me. I tried to outrun him, which I knew was stupid because he could run faster than I could. But I was hoping that the arrow would slow him down. I reached a large tree and started to climb it. Since the bear had been running, he had lost a lot of blood and didn't have the strength to climb up after me. He faltered and fell backward. I jumped down and cut his throat, and he died instantly. I brought the bear back, in the traditional tribal way, with my brothers, to my tribe. My parents were very proud of me, a young boy, for killing such a ferocious animal. There was a big celebration to welcome me into the tribe but this time I could stand as equal to the other braves. I was very proud. I enjoyed the pat on the back and my ego was a bit inflated from thinking that I was a great warrior.

A year or two went by and I, then fifteen years old, was listening outside the elders' tipi. They were discussing what to do about the white man, in particular, the soldiers who were building a camp about a day's ride from our village. They didn't know what to do about them. Hearing this, I thought I could do something to help my people. I wanted to be the hero again. I went out on my own and walked until I came to the white man's fort. I went alone and offered them beads as a peace offering. With the help of an interpreter, I told them they didn't have anything to fear because my people didn't want any trouble and were confident that his people were willing to live in peace with us. They said, "Yes, yes, now be a good lad and go back and tell your chief that we mean him no harm and that all is well."

I went back feeling pretty good about what I had done and told the chief that they were friendly. He became outraged. "You crazy boy! You could have been killed," he shouted. He told me never to go out alone again without consulting him first. The arrangement I had negotiated seemed to work out for a while, however, the chief eventually began to notice more and more white people moving into the fort. They were cutting down more and more trees and hunting farther and farther out in order to feed all of the new people. The chief was worried that his tribe would not have enough food to get through the winter.

I asked to go and speak with the white man again and tell them to not go into our hunting grounds. The chief agreed but sent another brave along with me. This time, we did not bring gifts. This time it was strictly business. I had to be firm and tell them not to go into our sacred hunting ground.

The white man agreed to be more careful. Several more seasons passed and little by little, they continued to go into the restricted territory. I still felt that the white man could be trusted and that the intruder must be some rogue hunter. But the chief was not happy. He was very leery about what was going on. I felt that the white man would ultimately honor the agreement. We waited. This waiting period was very tense. We watched more closely. The chief was worried that his people might not have enough food to get through the winter, and the question became, "Should we move to a better hunting ground?" By this time, the people were convinced that the white man did not care about them and they didn't want to move because they believed that if they moved, they would have to move again and again until there was no place left to go. The chief called a council. He said that the people must stand and fight the white man and tell him he couldn't run them off their land.

"No! You don't understand. They have strong weapons; we cannot fight them. I have seen their firearms, and our arrows are no match for them. There are too many of them. They will wipe us out," I pleaded.

"You can either stand with us or you can go and join with them. If you don't want to fight with us, then we don't want you," the chief replied.

I became frantic. I didn't know what to do. I didn't want to see my family die. I was sure they would not be able to stand up to the white man. In a panic, I left, determined to make one more attempt to save them from the worst disaster ever. I was not afraid to fight; I just didn't want to see all of my people die. I ran to the white man's camp to speak with them. I wanted to be the hero and save my people. I told them my people were coming to fight them if they didn't stop this advance on our hunting ground. It was their last chance. The chief was fed up with their promises and wanted them to leave. The white man laughed and said they wanted to fight because they needed our land and this was the only way to settle it. They tied me to a tree. I was furious. I felt stupid for ever having believed them. I should have listened to my chief, I should have known that the white man lied, I should have stayed to fight with my brothers. I thought, now I have to watch as my brothers are slaughtered.

As I saw them coming closer, I cried out, "My brothers, let me fight with you!" Then, just before my brother was shot off of his horse, he took aim and shot an arrow right through my heart. I was in agony, feeling that I had let my brothers down and was now going to die as an outcast in the hands of the enemy. I died thinking I was an outcast, full of shame.

In the Bardo

In the Bardo, I cried and cried and hung my head in shame. I saw the chief and told him how sorry I was and that the chief was right. I admitted that one cannot reason with cheats and liars, and it is better to stand together with one's brothers than to die alone in the hands of the enemy. In that life, I had been mistaken in thinking I could be a hero. My ego was too big and I wanted to save everyone. In my pride, I forgot to pray and ask the Great Spirit for guidance. If I had done that, I would have known what to do. In the Bardo, the chief came to me and asked, "What is it that you want?"

"Please take me back, please forgive me. Please take me back. I don't want to be an outcast for all eternity," I implored him.

The chief told me to go to the mountaintop, pray for forgiveness from the Great Spirit, and ask the ancestors to come and help me. My mother came and pleaded on my behalf, saying I was misguided by pride but had meant well. The chief sent me off to pray.

I fasted and prayed and asked the Spirit for guidance. An eagle came and gave me sight to see the truth in all matters. I could now see the big picture that I couldn't before. After three days, I returned to my people. I said to the chief, "I have seen the truth and the truth confirms that my people were right to stand together and fight for what they believed in. It was the honorable thing to do. I now know that the white man is the great deceiver." Then they welcomed me back and celebrated in their new village in the Bardo. At that time, I called the other brave who had shot and killed me. We forgave each other. "I felt your anger," he said. "I would have done the same thing if I had been you." Now we could hug each other and celebrate our unity.

Next, I called in the lieutenant from the fort. The man was a decorated hero in his land for wiping out so many native people, but I told him that the spirit of the native people would follow him, his children, and his children's children until they learned to live in peace and harmony with the earth and all the people who dwelt in it. They must repent for what they had done against the mother earth. Until they learned to live in peace, they would never find peace. I sent him away to learn what truth is and how to take care of the mother earth.

In this lifetime, the brother who shot me with the arrow is my brother today.

Here is a chart of what I've uncovered thus far. I am astonished now because I thought I was learning so much and doing so well, but clearly, I still have a lot to learn. Being afraid of crowds isn't such a huge obstacle; it's just something I have to learn to deal with. The things I'm concerned with are telling lies, not being heard, fear of deprivation, and shame and guilt. I feel that I have met the complex of truth head on. I have seen it from both sides: lying to the authorities, lying to the master, and being lied to. Being caught and having to face the resulting shame taught the slave boy and the young Englishwoman who lost her life a significant lesson. Although the Englishwoman sacrificed herself for a greater good, the love of her daughter, she still lied.

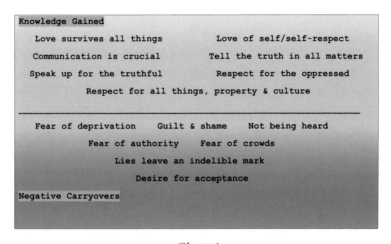

Knowledge Gained

Love survives all things	Love of self/self-respect
Communication is crucial	Tell the truth in all matters
Speak up for the truthful	Respect for the oppressed
Respect for all things, property & culture	

Fear of deprivation   Guilt & shame   Not being heard

Fear of authority   Fear of crowds

Lies leave an indelible mark

Desire for acceptance

Negative Carryovers

Chart 1

The greatest knowledge, however, came to the Native American brave, who felt the sting of being lied to. He jeopardized his entire tribe for a false belief. This brave seems to be the counterbalance to the Englishwoman who lied; even though her reason for lying was a noble one, she still lied and caused her own demise. The Native American boy had to do a lot of soul-searching in the Bardo to be accepted back into the tribe. He gave up his ego to learn an important lesson.

Not being heard was the last thing I was left holding in my psyche in the second chapter. Therefore, in the next chapter, I want to see whether I address it in subsequent lifetimes.

CHAPTER THREE

LET THE BODY TELL THE STORY

The body is but a temporal respite for the soul. In the Tibetan philosophy, the body only houses the soul, and each new incarnation takes on a new body. Everything that happens to us in this lifetime or any other lifetime is recorded in the etheric field. All memories are embedded in the subtle body. The etheric field is the first layer of the subtle body, which surrounds the physical body and fills a space of about six inches around the body. It carries the imprints from past lives. It is also known as the qi, prana, or life force of an individual. This energy never dies and is always available to us, but when it is blocked by unresolved issues or trauma, the energy cannot flow properly and will lead to disease and dysfunction. Each incarnation will leave imprints which continue to influence us.

What I was taught through the training I received from Dr. Woolger is that physical ailments, especially those that can't be explained, are usually imprints from other lifetimes. When I interview a new client, I ask questions about illnesses, accidents, physical ailments, and so on. I'm looking to discover any physical condition that could be an entry point into a story. I will also want to know at what age the incident happened. It is interesting to note that triggers in this lifetime are often tied to incidences that happened in past lives. I just recently did a regression with a young woman who suffered from migraine headaches. The headaches seemed to have started after a serious car accident. Through the regression, she discovered that in a past life she had had her head bashed in at the same age that she had the car accident in this lifetime. Is it coincidental that the headaches were a symptom in both lives?

I will often focus on a client's bodily pain or discomfort to get into a story line from a past life. For example, if a client comes to me with a pain in her back, I will explore the pain and ask for a description of what the pain is like – sharp, dull, throbbing, and so on. I will continue to probe by asking the client for more specifics. The client will continue to explore it by saying something like, "It feels like something is pushing into my back at this particular spot."

"Go on," I'll say. "What is pushing into it?"

"It feels like something cold and sharp," the client may say. I will continue in this manner until we come to an exact description of the object used to pressure or puncture the back. Eventually, this line of questioning will reveal a story. An image will surface, such as the point of a bayonet pushing him or her forward. That image is enough to lead us into a story. The objective is to get to the point of remembering that in fact in a past life the client was stabbed in the back with a bayonet. It is important to remove the phantom object. The bayonet must be removed and the wound needs to be healed in order for the pain to be released.

There can be layers to the story on both the physical and emotional levels, which will contribute to the imprint on the psyche resulting from the back pain that is still manifesting in the present day.

You may be wondering how I can bring you to remember an event that happened so long ago. Because the imprint of the memory is in the etheric field of your subtle body, when you relax and focus, you can ask your body to tell the story behind the pain in your back. Images will emerge from your unconscious. Some practitioners use hypnosis to get their clients into the relaxed state necessary to access this memory, but I prefer to use a relaxed state referred to as an alpha state.

In this state of meditation, the client is fully awake, but can still access feelings and impressions from the physical body.

Hypnosis is a trance state characterized by extreme suggestibility, relaxation, and heightened imagination, somewhere between Alpha and Theta.

Levels

1. Beta is fully awake.
2. Alpha is light meditation or daydreaming, a bridge between conscious and unconscious states.
3. Theta is just below alpha, more like a sleep state.
4. Delta is associated with deep sleep.

As stated before, I prefer that my clients stay in the Alpha state so that they can remember what they are thinking and feeling. When a client starts to slip into the Theta state, I can bring their awareness back to the body by dramatizing the action of the story. Often, I will ask the client to show me exactly how the body was held; for example, the arm was bent a particular way or the foot was crushed under a rock. Then I will apply slight pressure on the foot, which will bring the awareness there, and so on. When someone is in the Alpha state, the slightest touch will draw their focus to the subject at hand. In this way, the body wakes up and remembers what was going on physically, emotionally, and mentally.

This next regression is also about truth; half-truths are still lies, so no matter how one tries to rationalize it, a lie is a lie and will follow its creator.

Dutch Explorer, The New World (Late 1600's)

I have a scar on my lower abdomen, a reminder of three surgeries. I was curious about why I had to have three surgeries in exactly the same place and was determined to get to the root cause. The hook I used for this regression was the fear left in the solar plexus. The past life practitioner and I entered the scene with me, as a man, crawling on my belly, holding my guts in, trying to get back to my village. Evidently, I had been mauled by a bear and had to hold myself together until I could get help. I managed to get back to the village, where my wife took care of me and helped nurse me back to health.

How did this happen? I was a Dutchman who was hired to track for fur in the new world. It seemed to be somewhere along the Virginia coast within an English settlement. I had a very good reputation for tracking not only animals but also Native Americans. I was hired to negotiate with the natives and convince them that the trappers were honorable and only wanted to trade with them. I knew all along that that was only half the truth that more and more Europeans would be coming to the new world to settle on Native American Territory. I was basically opening the door for more white people to come in.

After the bear attack, I had to recuperate for the entire winter. When the spring came, however, I was back out, leading a group of men to hunt and trap. We had traveled far from home one day and found ourselves surrounded by a Native tribe I didn't know. I tried to talk my way out of the situation, but I knew that my men and I had wandered into uncharted territory. The natives could sense that I was not telling them the truth about their intentions and they killed me and my entire group. I died feeling like a total fraud, having lied to the Native Americans and led my men into a fatal ambush. I was filled with guilt, especially since they had hired me as an expert in affairs of this sort.

In the Bardo

The bear had tried to show me (by attacking me in the gut) that my fear in the belly was there because I was weak and dishonest, not only to the Native Americans but to the English as well. I was a yellow belly. I died in shame and I knew all along that I was deceitful. But I explained in the Bardo that I was hired by the English to do a job: to help establish a new settlement. I knew I had lied to the Natives, but that was what I was being paid to do. What I hadn't bargained for was leading my men into an ambush. I thought the intrigue of trinkets would be enough to settle the boundary issue. I had underestimated the integrity of the indigenous people and paid dearly for it. I suppose the lesson in that lifetime was to always be aboveboard and speak the whole truth rather than half-truths. I died a fool and my men lost their lives because they believed I would be able to negotiate with the natives. Oddly enough, in the Bardo, they didn't seem to hold me accountable for it but agreed that I had miscalculated the Native American integrity. None of us had known how the natives felt about commerce versus territory and we were all new at dealing with the locals.

How does the Dutchman regression relate to this life? I have had surgery on this part of my abdomen on three different occasions. In a way, having these surgeries done on my abdomen was addressing the complex of not being true to oneself. Bear is about setting sound boundaries. It is no wonder that she showed up in this story. This explorer did his job but had no integrity. The native people could sense that right away. Doubtless this story was literally about setting territorial boundaries, but it was also about setting boundaries with oneself. Even if you are hired to do a job, in this case to trap for a fur trading company, it doesn't serve you well to lie in order to get what you want. The Native Americans were constantly taken for fools who would cower for rewards of trinkets and material possessions. This was a very European concept with no integrity or honor. They totally underestimated the native people. It's no wonder that I have no stomach for that sort of thinking today.

I learned this lesson the hard way. The young Russian girl had integrity, and so did the Englishwoman who would not cave into monetary pressures. But the slave boy was desperate and would have done anything to change his state in life. As we have seen in these regressions, property and territory seem to have a great influence on one's integrity. Respect for a people's ideology, bodies, and possessions seem to all be tied together with the natural world. I think the land is only a manifestation of our own thoughts and deeds. Bear showed up to define the meaning of boundary. The young girl in the new world story learned that one can't just take what one wants because there are boundaries.

The stomach is also a symbol of the solar plexus; the solar plexus chakra is the energy center associated with ego. This is the source of personal power, self-belief, and self-worth. This man lost his power because he had no integrity. He was living a lie. The Englishwoman also lost her feminine power in the torture chamber, not only because she lied but because the men at that time were afraid of the feminine power and had to keep it in check. She was compelled to commit to her story to survive; if she had given in to their pressure and given them the money she had hidden, they would only have come back again and again, each time looking for more. She tried to set a boundary, saying "enough is enough." I think there is something to be said for speaking one's truth as a woman and not being heard because one is not seen as a valuable contributor to the greater good. As in the story of the Russian girl, women have not been heard for centuries. This is nothing new. I also feel that women have had to go within to find their own source of power and work in subliminal ways to hold on to it.

Our journey continues, exploring the body and how it holds stories of our past. I was lucky enough to have this shown to me by the expert in the field of parapsychology. In this next session, Roger Woolger used me in a demonstration for the teaching module "Let the Body Tell the Story" before a group of students in 2009.

The Pecking Order (Portuguese boy Late 1500s)

To start my regression, Dr. Woolger asked me to draw a picture of my body and highlight the areas that felt restricted, tense, painful, or irritated, or had some kind of discomfort. Next, he asked me to associate feeling words to the area. I had wanted to uncover the problem with my kidneys since I had nephrosis as a kid. I felt that my kidneys hadn't fully developed when nephrosis set in because I was born premature at only three pounds.

Words I used to describe the feeling in my kidneys included *hard, stiff, achy, immobile, yellow, and sickly, exhausted, stressed*, and *throbbing*.

Then Dr. Woolger asked me to associate an image with the pain or feeling. It seemed that there was pressure from something, that my kidneys were shaken, banged, damaged, almost as if they were hit by a piece of wood.

This was the concrete image that Dr. Woolger used to go into a scene. As I perceived the wood hitting me in the back, I felt myself running in the sand, trying to get away, tripping because I was running so fast, and not being able to get up because they kept hitting me with this piece of driftwood. This scene was reenacted with Roger and Patricia (his assistant) hitting my back as I tried to get up. But they kept knocking me down, over and over again, until I just couldn't get up anymore. Finally, my attackers left me alone.

Dr. Woolger then proceeded to ask about the person lying on the beach. I'm a young man of 18 or 19 years of age. Are you a slave boy? No. Who are you? I'm a sailor. Are you part of an exploring ship? Yes. British? No. Portuguese, I'm a Portuguese boy. How did you get to be a sailor on the ship? Let's go back to the beginning. How did this all come about?

Do you have a family? Yes, I have a mother and father. Where are they? They are in a fishing village. Is your father a sailor? No, he owns a restaurant.

I could see the tables in the restaurant with windows that opened up to the port. I could see the boats moored at their docks and hear the seagulls. There were windows with blue shutters and wooden tables and chairs and a lively group of men that had just come into port having beers at the bar. My mother was in the kitchen cooking and we had a wonderful fish stew that she offered to the men. I was young, a boy of about seven or eight. I waited on the tables and brought the men their beer, running back and forth from table to table. I loved to come to the restaurant and help my parents. I couldn't wait to hear all the men's stories when they came back from their trips to far off places. There was one man in particular who came in all the time. He didn't go out to sea anymore because he was old, but he had so many stories of traveling around the world, of pirates and strange cultures from the Orient and the islands. I loved to hear him tell me stories and couldn't wait for the day that I could travel like he did and be a sailor.

Finally, the day came when I turned 18. This man introduced me to a sea captain and asked him if he needed a deckhand, an apprentice to take with him on his next voyage. He agreed to take me under his wing and brought me on board as the new deckhand and gofer to clean and help in the kitchen. I was the youngest one on the ship and the other sailors made fun of me because I didn't know anything about sailing. But I knew how to cook and clean and that was fine with them as long as I stayed out of their way.

I was so excited to be going out to sea. My parents were happy for me because this was what I had always dreamed of, but a little sad because I was their only son and they would miss me terribly. I mostly kept to myself when I wasn't working and had a bunk in the bottom of the ship near the storage rooms. No one bothered me and I tried to keep out of their way, but I wanted to learn everything about sailing. The captain was the nicest to me and tried to explain things to me, but he was always busy and didn't have a lot of time for me. We were headed toward the Caribbean islands and I couldn't wait to see them. I had heard so much about them, but so far all I saw was sea in every direction. Then, one night, the captain decided to change course to avoid an approaching storm. The sailors thought it would be best to sail through the storm head-on. It would be rough, they thought, but the wind at their backs would help them to push through and lessen the storm's effects. But the captain was adamant that we would turn and go around it. It came down to a vote, and since I didn't know anything about sailing and the captain was my only friend on the ship, I decided to side with him. The other sailors were mad at me because they couldn't overturn the captain's ruling without a unanimous vote, but I trusted the captain. After all, it was his ship and he had more experience than they did.

The storm came and, as it turned out, a tremendous backwind caught our ship as we tried to circumvent the storm. It caught the crew off guard and turned the ship into a splintered mess, running its remains aground on a small beach in the outer Antilles, West Indies.

I survived the storm, but we lost a lot of men and the ship was destroyed. The men who were left made it to the small island and were pretty shaken up by what had happened. As they talked, they became enraged when they saw me and began yelling at me, saying it was my fault. If they had gone the other way, this wouldn't have happened. They shook their fists at me, and one man said, "I ought to beat your brains in." He came after me with a piece of driftwood he found on the beach. I started to run, but the sand was hot, and my feet were burning. He hit me in the back with the wood. I ran as far as I could, but the blows to my back were hard and kept knocking me down. Finally, I fell, and the men just kept hitting me. I cried and told them I was sorry, that I didn't know, that I hadn't meant to cause the shipwreck. I begged them to stop and leave me alone. Finally, I was too weak to fight them anymore, and they left me there in the heat, exhausted and bleeding.

My back was swollen, and I was lying face down in the sand, hoping the sun would go down so I could rest and find some water. But then the buzzards came. First, they circled around, but then they converged and began pecking at me. I cried and screamed, but I was too weak to move. They kept coming and pecking, and eventually pecked at my back and ate my kidneys and innards until I was dead and couldn't scream anymore.

In the Bardo

In the Bardo, I cried and cried. I let all my anguish and disappointment out. I said to the crew, "I wanted to be like you. I wanted to see the world and learn everything about sailing. Why did you hate me so much? What did I do?" The crew said they blamed me for what had happened even though the outcome would have probably been the same either way. They were so angry that they had lost their friends, their cargo, and their ship, which was their livelihood, and they took it out on me. They didn't want to kill me, they just wanted to teach me a lesson. They scapegoated me and blamed the buzzards, rather than themselves, for my death.

I summoned Candor, who had been called in to fight off the birds and stand guard to protect me. A healer was called in to restore my kidneys and an old sea captain came, stood shoulder to shoulder with me, and supported my decision to side with the captain. The captain came and said he respected and honored me and told the crew to leave me alone. They could have taught me many things. I was eager and willing to learn. The captain chastised the crew for being so blinded by their own frustration and taking it out on a simple boy who only wanted to emulate them and learn from them. The entire crew was sent to anger management sessions and training to learn compassion in the Bardo. They were also stripped of their titles. I was able to stand my ground and tell the crew how I felt.

I was at the bottom of the pecking order in this situation, but I didn't deserve what they had done to me. I was innocent. In the Bardo, I was given an honorable burial at sea, the kind that was ordered for respected sailors, so I could regain the respect I deserved.

This relates to current life situations in that this pecking order phenomenon has been present in every single work situation I've ever been in. Being an artist usually means being out of the norm, different. This is true in the workplace as well as in society. Try to get a bank loan as an artist or look at the pay scale for art related positions; they are usually in the lower quarter of the workforce, unless, of course, you are famous. Then you get all the attention and accolades. Being an art therapist seemed to follow suit. In the workplace, I was at the bottom of the rankings of importance to the network. After this regression, things at my last job did improve. It wasn't dramatic, but at least I got more respect from coworkers.

Physically, I felt much better. My kidneys seemed to function better. I had more energy and was able to work out more than I had previously. I had less water retention in my legs and less puffiness under my eyes.

Being at the bottom of the pecking order seems to resonate with me, and fitting in has always been a struggle for me. Not feeling like I belong to the group is something I still struggle with. I have a need to prove myself and want to be perfect so no one will be able to find fault with me. I don't want to be at the bottom of the totem pole. Not that I have to be at the top, either, but somewhere in the middle would be just fine, and to be accepted by my peers would be inspiring.

In the real world, the way this played out is interesting. Having owned a restaurant with my husband for 12 years, I encountered all kinds of people. I ran the kitchen, which came naturally to me even though I had no previous experience. There was a man named Daniel who came into our restaurant all the time. He lived locally and was one of the engineers who designed the Tappan Zee Bridge. He used to come in for lunch, and after the rush was over, I would come out from the kitchen to sit with him. He was a great storyteller and was well traveled. I enjoyed his company and his stories. After a while, we became friends and I told him about a show at a local gallery I was having of my paintings. He was very interested and came to the opening. He purchased this painting, entitled *Costa Amalfi*.

This was a simple painting I did in Sorrento, Italy. It showed the view from our balcony at the hotel where my husband and I stayed. Daniel purchased the painting because he said it reminded him of the view from his boat that he kept in the harbor in (of all places) Lisbon, Portugal. Evidently, Daniel owned a condo in Lisbon and was planning to retire there.

Figure 7: Costa Amalfi oil on canvas by G. C. De Pietro

You could say this is coincidental, or you could say that Daniel was the sailor who used to come into the restaurant that was owned by the boy's family in the story. My husband and I sold our restaurant in 1986. This regression was in 2009, 23 years after my interaction with Daniel. I didn't even make the connection until weeks after the regression when I was writing about it and that warm, fuzzy feeling of familiarity came over me. That is when I remembered sitting at the bar, listening to Daniel's stories. I hope to get to Lisbon someday to see the old fishing villages there. I'm not at all interested in going to the Caribbean islands, however, or the Antilles, for that matter.

As far as my kidneys go, I have no idea why this particular ailment would surface in this lifetime. I do feel that there was a reason I experienced a deathly illness in my childhood. I have been made aware of the unseen world because of having been so close to death in my youth. It has set me on this life's journey and is perhaps the reason for this exploration into past lives. I have come to believe that nothing happens randomly and there is a reason for everything.

This demonstration was a very good example of how we can use the body to remember past life events. Dr. Woolger was a master at it and it was a marvel to watch him work with clients, particularly resistant clients who were afraid to remember or didn't believe in the process. Dr. Woolger was able to find the thread of truth that opened the door into the psyche and allowed the process to unfold.

How does this story relate to the other stories? The Portuguese boy was young and naïve, honest and open, not like the slave boy, who was cunning and deceitful, but more like the girl who had to run from the natives in the early American story. Even though these children were young and seemingly innocent, their souls carried many imprints. This young boy may have had a debt to pay to these other sailors, so his naïveté didn't give him a pass to skirt his payback. There was nothing in this boy's life that could have prepared him for what happened to him. We will continue to probe other stories to see how this karma plays out.

The Dutch Explorer story seemed to address the guilt and shame issue that has come up. Lies follow those who tell them. As we have seen several times now, even a half-truth might as well be a lie. There is no way around it. Weakness and fear are reflected in the Englishwoman's story as well as the slave boy. The Dutchman could not have ignored the lesson the bear showed him. It was all about setting sound boundaries and telling the truth.

As far as the Portuguese boy is concerned, the desire for acceptance was tantamount. He was able to work some of this out in the Bardo by receiving a proper burial at sea reserved for honored sailors. He got some sense of being accepted. We will see if this sort of thing continues to surface in subsequent lifetimes, but as far as this lifetime goes, things did change at work for me. I established better communication between myself and the administration.

The next three regressions were done as an independent study with a colleague after the workshop had ended. Using the body as a way of entering into a story line was how my subconscious was able to bring my awareness to information that needed to be addressed. My colleague and I traded sessions as we both had issues we wanted to work out.

Nancy, England, (Mid-1700s)

I had gone sailing the week before this session and gotten a cold sore on my mouth. What ended up happening was that my lips blew up and there were blisters all around the edges. I guess I developed an aversion to sailing after the Portuguese sailor life. It was difficult even to talk when I arrived at the session. When my colleague, Val, asked me how my swollen mouth felt, I said that it felt as if someone had punched me in the mouth. Letting the body tell the story, Val reenacted the scene of someone beating me, imitating blows to the head as I tried to protect myself. As Val struck me I repeatedly told him to stop. He kept yelling at me, saying, "You'll do as I say, and I'll beat you until you learn not to disobey me."

"Where are you?" she asked. "Can you see where this is taking place?"

Yes. I was a young woman named Nancy, attractive but poor. A man was holding me in some sort of garret and had beaten me so badly I could hardly move. Finally, he left me, and I rested on the floor. The door was locked, and he had something tied around my ankle, so I couldn't move far from the bed, but I managed to get to a window. Down in the street, I saw a finely dressed woman just stepping out of a carriage. I banged on the window until she looked up, and she screamed in horror when she saw my bloodied face. I pleaded with her, "Please help me. Please help me." She ran to get a police officer and pointed up to the window, saying, "There! There is a woman who is badly beaten up there." The officer came with several other men. They broke the door down and took me to the hospital. I told them about the man who had done this to me. Evidently, it was my boyfriend, and he had threatened to kill me if I said anything. They sent out an alert and took dogs to go find the culprit.

How did I get into this situation? What had I done to make the boyfriend so angry with me? It wasn't the first time that he had hit me, but I was afraid he would kill me, and I didn't want to go along with him anymore. He made a living by getting me to go to the local pub to flirt with fellows and suggest that I would go home with them. At the end of the night, I would invite them back to my place, but instead, I would lead them down a dark alley where my boyfriend would corner them. Since they had been drinking all night, they would be no match for him, and he would rob them. But one night a fellow put up a pretty good fight and Taylor, the boyfriend, hit him over the head with a club. I found out later that the man had died from his injuries. After that, I told Taylor that I wouldn't do it anymore, that it was too violent, and that sooner or later we would be discovered.

That is when he took me to the apartment and beat me. But at this point, it didn't matter, because if I continued to do his dirty work, I would eventually get in trouble with the law. Even if I didn't, he would kill me, so I was in a no win situation. The police were looking for the man who had killed a prominent businessman in the community. When I told them about the plot and about Taylor, they believed me because he had been in trouble many times before. I stayed in the hospital long enough to recuperate and then was released to go home. I had planned to get my things and leave town, but of course, Taylor was waiting for me.

When he saw me, he grabbed me and choked me for betraying him. Ultimately, I didn't care because I couldn't live that life anymore and I knew I would have the last word – they would find him, and justice would be served. I was still afraid of him, though, and died feeling betrayed by him, the man I had loved. I knew then that he had never really loved me, but merely used me to make money for himself.

In the Bardo

I met Taylor in the Bardo and told him he couldn't control me anymore. He was still angry with me and blamed me for his arrest and conviction. He was still trying to control me, even in the Bardo. I told him that it was really over, and he couldn't control me anymore. He needed serious rehab work and anger management classes. He had no respect for women, which was his basic problem, and he needed to work on that. I called in my Angels to stand with me as I faced my abuser, and they took him away to learn respect and compassion. They gave me the strength to face him. I also called in the woman I had seen from the window. I wanted to thank her again for helping me. Oddly enough, she had some connection to the man Taylor had killed in the alleyway. She was a sister or cousin or something to him. This regression seems to balance out the lies and the half-lies of my other lives, as Nancy went to great lengths to tell the truth about what she and Taylor were doing to unsuspecting men.

In relation to this life, the man named Taylor in the regression is my present-day brother, who bullied me when we were growing up and controlled me through fear tactics, just like my dad. After the regression, I realized this was an old story that I've been carrying for a long time. I have always been afraid of my father and my brother because they were bullies. I had terrible nightmares about them coming and hurting or killing me. This story was about boundaries, bullying, standing my ground, and reclaiming my (feminine) power. These themes play out in subsequent stories, but in that lifetime, I just needed to protect myself.

This next regression has a lot to do with not being heard and yet another boundary issue.

Adam, Logger, (Rural America 1800s)

Using a body memory, I told Val (DMP ® Practitioner) that I felt like my teeth were broken and rotten. We used this imprint to get into the story line, again letting the body lead us into a scene. I entered a one-room schoolhouse. I was Adam, a young boy about 12 years old. I was one of the older boys in the school and I was a real cutup. The teacher had had it with me that day and gave me a smack on the head for being loud and disruptive. She kicked me out of class and told me not to return. I arrived home in the middle of the day and my mother was furious when I told her that the teacher didn't want me to come back. She beat me upside the head some more and told me I had to get a job. She was home with an infant, a three-year-old, and a five-year-old. My father was not around; he had left us. He had gone off to find work but never returned to the family, so we had to get on the best we could.

So, as a young boy of 12, I had to go find work. I found a logging community not far from home that was always looking for extra hands. It was hard work, but I had to take it to help the family. Several years went by and I became restless. I remembered a girl named Becky from school that I liked, and I wanted to take her out. I called on her a few times and she seemed to like me as well, but as soon as my mother found out, she was furious with me. "Don't we have enough mouths to feed around here without you bringing home some girl and getting her pregnant and adding to the mess we're already in?" she demanded. I was heartbroken that I had to stop calling on this girl. The next thing I knew, she had run off with someone else. I continued to work and bring home the money but fell into despair. By this time, I was in my early twenties and all I ever did was work. I started going out and drinking with the guys after work. It seemed to be the only way I could drown my loneliness. My mother began to yell at me for drinking, saying that I was going to be just like my father. My teeth began to rot from all the drinking. This was the last straw for me. One day, I got into a bitter fight with my mother and struck her. We continued in this uneasy way for some time but my drinking, and our fighting, grew worse until one day I felt like killing her, I was so angry with her. I had given up my whole life for my family and had no life of my own. Feeling unappreciated and worthless, I took my anger out on my mother, telling her this wasn't the life I wanted. I threatened to leave them. She yelled back, saying, "Go ahead and be just like your father. Leave us here to starve. Be the good-for-nothin' that I know you are." I attacked her. She lifted a heavy cast-iron skillet from the stove and brought it down on my head. My teeth fell out as I hit the floor, never to get up again. I died feeling like a workhorse whose only job was to provide for my siblings with no joy in my life.

In the Bardo

As Adam, I died in a drunken stupor, so in the Bardo, my first task was to clear the alcohol from my system. I called in a doctor to help me with the bandages on my head and with my teeth, most of which were rotten from the drinking or broken from the fatal blow. I called in my mother next. I talked with her about why she had been so cruel to me. Evidently, she had been raised in a very poor household and married young because her mother couldn't afford to feed her anymore. As soon as she was married, however, she began having babies of her own and found herself in the same situation as her mother. But her situation was even worse because she had a husband who abandoned her, leaving her with four mouths to feed. She had never had any joy in her life and felt trapped. Her only son, who could have helped her, was an abusive drunk to her, and she couldn't stand another day of that life. She felt sorry that I didn't have a life, but there was no joy in her life either. Instead of working together toward a common goal, we fought, which only made matters worse. I began to understand how my life was a mirror of misery to my mother's. For the first time, I felt sorry for her. But I couldn't forgive her for the way she had spoken to me and abused me after all I had sacrificed for her and her children.

In the Bardo was the first time we had ever talked about how we got into our situation. Our limited experience had never allowed us to explore possible solutions. In the Bardo, we could imagine what our lives might have been like if we had chosen a different outcome. Although my mother needed some interventions, I felt it was not my place to tell her how to fix her problems. She was sent away to learn problem solving and constructive communication skills instead of fighting as a way to resolve disagreements.

I was still longing for my girlfriend Becky, whom I was now able to call in. She had married the other fellow only because if she hadn't, she would have become an old maid, but she confessed that I was her true love. I was able to find the joy I had missed in that lifetime. As Adam, all I had ever wanted to do was take my pretty girl to the dance, show her off, have fun, and be held and loved by her. We left Adam in the Bardo with Becky to experience a young and carefree life with the girl of his dreams.

What lessons were learned? Adam learned that he could discuss and negotiate situations and didn't have to take verbal or physical abuse from anyone. His mother had held him in a subservient role using guilt as a motivator. Adam realized this didn't work and only created resentment. He learned that guilt could be changed to love and compassion and that through thoughtful planning, dire situations could be avoided.

This relates to my life today because my mother in this life was my mother in the story. She always seemed to want to party and have a social life. She married young, her marriage was abusive, and she felt trapped (sound familiar?). She always felt she was missing out on life and she was driven to have a good time. After having reviewed this past life, I understood her. I carried a lot of guilt as a kid, feeling that it was my job to try to make her happy. But as I got older, I realized I was only trying to make her happy so I wouldn't feel guilty about causing her to be unhappy (like Adam, who felt an obligation to fix his mother's problems). I suppose it would be a good idea to go back into the Bardo and help her to find happiness somehow, but it's not my place to discover her real joy. I can forgive her for causing so much pain in that rural American life, but I can't make her happy in this life or in the Bardo. That's something she will have to do for herself.

As Adam, I lacked the ability to tell her how unworthy and unappreciated she made me feel in that lifetime (not being heard). I have also felt underappreciated at work in this lifetime. It's vital to speak up and try to negotiate your position. Otherwise, resentment will build up, leading to anger and a belief that people don't appreciate your efforts. It became abundantly clear that festering resentment will eventually undermine a person, causing them to say and do things that are unnecessary.

As I mentioned before, I was very sickly as a child. The tetracycline the doctors prescribed for me caused my teeth to come in stained, showing ridges in the enamel after each high fever. So, as a teen, I had them all capped. Using my teeth as a body imprint led us into this story line. In the logger story, Adam's teeth were rotten and they all broke after he was hit in the face. This affliction may represent not being able to speak or speaking but not being heard. The character Adam tried to speak up for himself in this story, but it fell on deaf ears. Not being heard is one issue I seem to still be working out.

In the Bardo, Adam and his mother were able to come to an agreement. My mom in this life was a beautiful, gentle woman who I loved unconditionally and I'm sure she felt the same way about me. But there was an underlying sadness about her that no one was able to remedy. We had a much better relationship in this lifetime. I can see that she has been a teacher to me in many lifetimes. We will look at one more regression in this chapter to see how body imprints surface as carryovers from other lifetimes.

The Autistic Boy (Victorian Era, 1880s)

The induction method for this story was to use the migraine headache I was having and the need to shut out loud noises. As the eldest son of a prominent Victorian family, I was very sensitive to sound. I would become overwhelmed and deteriorate quickly when I was made to endure loud noises. The young woman who cared for me understood me better than anyone else in my family. She knew the only thing that would calm me down was being in nature. I could listen to the sounds of the birds, the wind through the trees, the ocean, and things like that to relax. I liked to be outside and to feel the sun on my skin. I could feel the vibration of the earth and I was one with it. My parents, on the other hand, could not handle the noises that I made and the rocking and the banging of my head, and they would punish me for being bad when all I wanted was to be left alone. They didn't understand the simple nature of my being. My father was embarrassed by me and wanted to ignore me. My mother didn't know how to deal with me and would leave me in my room to rock for endless hours.

Then one day, my baby sister started to cry. Her endless crying sent me into a frenzy. I picked up the baby, shook her, and banged her head on the ground until she stopped crying. I killed her, and everyone in the family went crazy with me. They had me put into a straitjacket and sent me away to a sanatorium. There, I was locked in a room where all I could do was rock and listen to the screams and wails of other inmates. I couldn't handle the noise; the echoes of the loud screams drove me insane and made my head hurt. To stop the noise and pain, I banged my head continuously until I split it open and died from the injury.

My mother cried because she felt such guilt. Why couldn't she help her little boy and relieve his suffering? My father was simply glad that it was all over; he felt that I had no place in their world. The nurse loved me and understood the pain I was in. She mourned my death.

In the Bardo

In the spirit world, I called in the Native American family, who understood that I was nurtured by nature and felt comfortable in the natural world. They demanded nothing of me and allowed me to just be present in nature. My purpose for this lifetime was to learn how to be in the moment, to give up fear as a thought that something bad might happen if I did this or that. I didn't understand cause and effect. I simply lived with no blame, no guilt, no worry about what might happen. I could not regulate the frequencies of sound and was overly sensitive to it.

I had the feeling that in between lives I lived in the Pleiadian world, where I became a sensitive and could pick up frequencies, traverse realms, and heal people through the frequencies. I was tortured by this knowledge, and the fear I experienced because of it was overwhelming. I came into the Victorian lifetime trying to not think about my powers but became overloaded by the slightest frequency because I was overly sensitive to it. I was still in shutdown mode and needed to just experience nature with no expectations of the powers that I possessed. I needed to totally surrender to the moment and just be. I forgave my family for not understanding me and apologized to my sister even though I hadn't known what I was doing, but had merely wanted the sound to stop. There was no blame and the baby understood that she couldn't be there for me because she was too young. I was just too sensitive for this world and needed a lot of special care.

It's interesting to note that the sister in this story was my mother in this present lifetime. The baby was killed by a distressed boy in that life for crying. I wonder if this had anything to do with the son she killed in the previous lifetime. Adam was angry enough with her to do something like that, so it is an interesting comparison. In this lifetime, I worked with autistic children for many years and can attest to the fact that loud noise is something they have a hard time filtering out. We have a much greater understanding of this condition today than they had in the Victorian era. I have great compassion for these children, which may stem from a deeper understanding gained by experiencing autism for myself in a past life.

Most Pleiadians I believe are sensitive to sound and frequency. Even today, I have to limit the amount of sound I hear. I need to have my own thoughts and feel most comfortable when surrounded by nature. It is possible that souls travel to other realms to learn and grow when they are asleep, while meditating, during guided imagery meditations or when they are not in the physical realm on this planet. Also, the concept of parallel lives theorizes that the soul can be in two places at one time which I have not personally experienced, but I don't think is beyond the realm of possibility.

The lesson here, in the Victorian life I think, was for others to learn how to accept one's limitations. I needed a respite from cognitive thought, as you will see. In a later regression, I was a learned professor who was brilliant but needed to rest his mind in that of the autistic boy. It was important that I learn to forgive and surrender, to give up fear, allow life to unfold, and abandon my expectations. Now is a time of acceptance, even for sensitives, to live in harmony with their abilities and their knowledge. It is safe to bring these out into the world now: empaths don't have to live in fear, or shut down, or hide their gifts.

Autistic people, I believe, are living in a different frequency from ours and they are frustrated in their inability to communicate their experiences to us. My hope is that as we evolve, we will be able to communicate on higher levels so that the autistic population can be understood and brought into the world more fully than they have been in the past.

CHAPTER FOUR

TRAUMA AND DISSOCIATION

All the practice sessions I was doing in regression work with my colleague were really helping me perfect my skills. I was becoming quite adept at finding the pathway into a story line. Once the story comes to its rightful completion, it's important to process the death scene and transition the spirit into the Bardo. There's no skirting around it. It's not enough to say, "Oh I had this wonderful life in Tahiti as a native. It was so utopian. I just loved it." You always need to ask why your psyche is showing you this lifetime. What was the lesson? Not all past lives end in trauma, so it's vital to remember your final thoughts during each death because the thought you hold when you die is the emotional and mental residue that will propel you into the next life. These last thoughts can also reveal what was unfinished for you in that life.

Often the trauma of a life can be so great that one dissociates, losing a part of him or herself, as in the story of Art, the soldier in Vietnam whom I wrote about earlier. When this happens to my clients, I may have to help them retrieve those lost bits of their soul, the parts that have splintered off. There is no telling where they may be hiding. Sometimes they hide in what the person in that life deemed as a safe place. Parts may go to a nurturing relative or the darkest corners of the universe. This retrieval process is very shamanic in nature and is usually not addressed in traditional therapeutic settings. Yet, it is a very real phenomenon. When you consider how vast your soul is and realize that you only incarnate with a fraction of it at any given time, it makes sense that you can't function well with missing parts. The part of your soul that does not incarnate with you is called your *higher self*.

How much of a soul is present in any given lifetime? I think, it depends on the person. I'm sure Jesus incarnated with most of his soul essence in his lifetime on earth; I would venture a guess of about 95 percent. Of course, you and I are mere mortals, so we would probably use only about 50 to 75 percent. A young man coming back from a war zone may only be functioning with about 25 percent of his soul; some of these soldiers could be characterized as the walking dead. It's funny how ubiquitous zombie movies are nowadays; this seems to speak to the truth about trauma and how so many of us are walking around with so little reserve. One doesn't have to be in a war zone to experience this. A variety of experiences or places of catastrophic earth change can bring about the same result. You never want to deplete your soul reserve or become an empty vessel. That's when unwanted spirits can take up residence, and it's also the reason I don't do drugs or drink much. It's never safe to give a wandering spirit a chance to enter your body or attach itself to you.

I am very aware of clients who are dissociated. If they come into the session that way, it is very difficult to work with them and I may have to do a soul retrieval first. During a session, if the character in the story becomes dissociated, I'll find them wandering around with no purpose or recall. It's important to retrieve those missing bits in order to properly process the story. Once those missing parts of a soul come back, the person will have much more energy, mental capacity, and stamina.

This next story is a very good example of a dissociated and traumatized individual. The term *shutdown moment* describes a point of trauma where one can lose a part of him or herself. The regression was performed in a workshop module during a level three Deep Memory Process® program with Dr. Woolger in 2010.

When an individual prepares for a regression, the psyche will start to percolate symptoms to the surface. I had been getting ready for the level three module for some time, and by the opening day of the workshop, I was ready. I was already starting to show signs of a story by the time I arrived. The unconscious knows what needs to be processed and will deliver it at just the right moment. This happens with clients that I book for sessions. I often tell them to pay attention to their dreams, mood changes, and physical symptoms as they get ready to come to see me. This is what happened with me in the story of the geisha girl.

Geisha Girl, Japan, 1600s

I had a feeling of trying to make myself invisible for days before the session.

I felt that if I laid very, very still and very quiet, it would be okay. I was a four-year-old little girl lying in a bed, hiding. Her parents were talking in the next room, making plans to take her somewhere. She was afraid. She thought that if she was very quiet and good, they would not find her in her bed and she would be able to stay with them. But they told her it would be a wonderful life. She would go to the best schools and get the best training in all of Japan.

This character (we'll call her Shinwa) was small and frightened and wanted to stay with her mommy. They came for her (shutdown moment), wrapped her up, and took her in a cart on a long journey to the temple in the big city. They left her there, and she was picked up and taken to a big house where many girls like her lived. She watched them and learned to imitate them, but she was too young to take the classes. So she worked around the house cleaning and washing and scrubbing the floors. It was very hard work, and her legs and feet hurt at the end of the day because she had to keep her feet wrapped very tightly with long white bandages.

There was one girl about her age that she became friendly with, named Shangshee. They were the best of friends and clung to each other because Shangshee also missed her family, especially her mother. They felt as if they had only each other. The big day finally came when they could enroll in the classes, and they started to learn the dances and songs that the geisha sang and performed. They also studied reading and writing because they had to become knowledgeable about the world.

Shinwa did very well with her lessons and worked very hard. She studied for many years and never complained. She was very happy to have her one friend to share secrets with. They helped each other cope and practiced together, perfecting their art in all areas. They learned to fix their hair and makeup professionally and dressed in the most beautiful kimonos. When the girls grew a little older, they went to the tea house for the first time together, and Shinwa found that she was shy with the young men and said little. However, she was very pretty and a good listener. She was polite and could always find the right answer when spoken to. They regularly performed and went to the tea house for several years. Shinwa was a popular performer. One very prominent man asked for her companionship, which was a great honor for her. He was a very powerful man. He was also a nice looking and pleasant man and seemed to be well bred. He spent more and more time with her and eventually she was only his companion.

They grew to know and like each other. Eventually, he asked to be her sponsor. She moved into a very nice house that he purchased for her. She had everything, fine china and beautiful clothes, whatever she wanted, because money was no problem for him. Shinwa tried very hard to please him, but she was unable to make him happy for some reason. At first, this was okay, but as time went on, he forbade her to sing or dance in public. She was only able to perform for him at small gatherings in their home. She hardly ever saw her friend Shangshee anymore. Only when she went to the market once a week did they meet, and if he had found out, he would have stopped that, too. He seemed to take away everything Shinwa loved and wanted her to focus only on him. She tried very hard to do the right thing, but over time, he became mean to her and beat her when he was upset. If he had a bad day or a fight with his wife, he took it out on her. Little by little, she secretly grew to hate him, and when he came to make love to her, she was mentally and emotionally absent (shutdown moment). She went through the motions but had no feelings for him.

One day, she discovered that she was pregnant and felt joy for the first time. She wanted to have a son to make her sponsor happy and to finally have a family she could love. He said nothing and didn't seem very happy about the news. Shinwa was overjoyed and couldn't wait to see her son. She had a baby boy and finally felt content and happy. What Shinwa didn't know was that her sponsor was making plans behind her back to give the boy away.

He came to her one day and told her she couldn't keep the baby. Shinwa was distraught. He said he already had a son and it would be a disgrace to his family name to have a bastard son with her. He gave the boy to his business partner, who had been trying unsuccessfully to have a son with his wife. Shinwa was beside herself with grief but unable to show her feelings; it was forbidden. She cried when she was alone, stopped eating, and became very depressed. She secretly met her friend Shangshee at the market, and the two girls planned to commit suicide together on the same night. They both felt there was no future for them, but at least they could be together in the afterlife. Shangshee obtained the poison from a vendor that she knew.

Shinwa went home to prepare herself. She fixed her hair and put on her best ceremonial dress. She lit candles and said her prayers, then drank the poison. She then laid down very still on the bed and waited for death to come. Her stomach burned and seized with cramps, and she was in great pain, but she didn't falter. She was committed to seeing it through. She wanted to be free. When she was dead, she flew up into the sky and looked for her friend Shangshee but did not see her. She flew to her friend's house and saw her crying in her room. Shangshee had heard the news about Shinwa's death and cried because she couldn't bring herself to keep their suicide pact. She cried because she had betrayed her friend's trust and because she was a coward.

Shinwa screamed when she found her friend still alive. She flew back to her own bedroom to find her sponsor there, screaming and yelling at her dead body. "I paid a lot of money for you," he screamed. "I gave you everything. How could you dishonor me this way?" Shinwa laughed and laughed, saying, "You thought you were so smart, but I get the last laugh because I outsmarted you. You can't control me anymore." Her sponsor refused to have her body cremated in the traditional ceremony, instead burying her in a common grave.

In the Bardo

In the Bardo, Shinwa called together all the geishas who had died in sorrow to celebrate their freedom and courage. They all honored her and she brought hundreds of geishas to the light. Shinwa also met with her parents, who told her how sorry they were for her life of sorrow. They didn't intend for her to have a sad life, and thought they were doing something special for her. Her grandmother was there, hugging her and saying how happy she was to have her back again. And her friend Shangshee came after a long, hard, painful life in which she was cast aside in her old age; she said, "If only I had the courage you had, I would have gone with you." Shinwa was also reunited with her son in the Bardo. He was never told that he was the son of a geisha, yet he always felt in his heart that he didn't fit in with his family. Somehow, he knew it wasn't right. He was happy to know the truth. He had been given a good life with his adopted family, and it relieved Shinwa to know that he was brought up well and cared for. All her pain was washed away in the Bardo.

When her sponsor came to her after he found out she was dead, he cried and screamed because for the first time, he realized how much he loved her. He never showed her his love in that lifetime because he had promised his wife that he would never love another woman. Now he was filled with guilt and remorse. He had held the most precious and beautiful woman in his hands. He was consumed by her and wanted to possess her. Shinwa did not try to reconcile her life with him in the Bardo; rather, she told him he couldn't possess her anymore. She was not an object, but a kind, sensitive, and beautiful person. He had to give up his obsession with her and learn to be caring and kind. She left him there to contemplate what he had done.

Shinwa had lead poisoning from the face paint that she wore, which may have led to even greater depression and irrational thought. She was healed in the Bardo and cleansed of the poison.

In my present lifetime, Shinwa's best friend Shangshee was my best friend in grade school, whom I vowed to be friends with forever. I cried and cried when she moved away, convinced that I would never have a better friend than her. The headmaster at the school, who took care of all the girls and sought perfection in all of them, was my mother in this life. The sponsor from that lifetime is a woman I know whose friendship with me is fraught with issues of control in this lifetime.

In relation to my present life:

The end of this regression was also the end of the weeklong workshop. At the end of every workshop, we would have a little celebration, acknowledge our accomplishments, and lighten the gravity of all our stories with fun and humor, great food and wine, and a lot of laughs. We ate and retired to the parlor, where we sometimes acted out our stories in a lighthearted and hilarious way. For some reason, I wasn't feeling well. The food I ate didn't settle right in my stomach, and I had only had one small glass of wine, but I begged off and said I was going to rest and that I would see everyone in the morning.

As the night went on, I became very sick. I don't think I detoxed enough during the regression. The entire night I vomited and suffered chills and dizzy spells. My friends checked on me, and I told them I expected to feel better by morning. But morning came, and I was still very sick. Everyone was leaving, and I tried to get up to say goodbye. Eventually, I was able to get back in my car and drive home, but I didn't feel well for several days. I think I had a visceral reaction to the poison Shinwa took in the story and my body was triggered into the terrible battle she had the night she died. It was an awful experience, and I learned to detox my clients in the Bardo thoroughly whenever the story line involved a drug or alcohol issue.

In this life, when I was in my mid-thirties, I was told I would be unable to have children because of a large tumor in my uterus. I went into a very deep depression and even became suicidal. That was the darkest period of my life, and it lasted about two months. I then went for a second opinion and luckily found a surgeon who could do the surgery I needed without any dire consequences. Thankfully, I have two beautiful girls today. But the age I had my fertility trouble in this lifetime was close to the same time in Shinwa's life that she had her child taken away from her.

I believe there's a parallel between the two scenarios. I feel that Shinwa's life encompassed my opposition to being controlled. I wanted to be my own person, something that is very evident in my life today. Shinwa was a very accomplished woman in the arts and in her ability to listen and comfort her clients. She was not prepared to accept the devalued position of mistress, especially one who had no rights or freedoms who was essentially a slave. That was not what she trained for, and it was not the life she was led to believe she would have. This took not being heard to a whole new level. By taking her life, she made a bold move that resonated in the afterlife.

In comparison to the other life stories, I think the theme of being a woman and not having any power is evident in the Englishwoman's life in the 1200s and that of the woman called Nancy, also in England. They all died thinking, "Enough is enough. I'm not going to take this anymore." It seems to me that throughout the ages, women and children have been used as property by the strong and powerful. This next story is very disturbing, and yet we know it still goes on in human trafficking today.

Clarissa and Rosa, Florence, Italy, 1500

As I mentioned before, my colleague Valerie and I had been trading sessions to improve our skills as (DMP) ® practitioners. I mention this regression I did for Valerie because while she was relaying her story, I realized I was part of that story as well. This memory was so vivid that I got caught up in its images because I was remembering it along with her. I drew these pictures after the regression because the imprint was just as strong for me as it was for her.

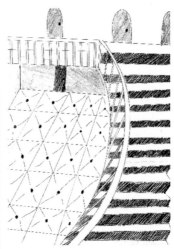

Figure 8: Front Foyer | *Figure 9: Stairs to Bedrooms*

Drawings by G.C. De Pietro

Regression therapy may be considered the extraction of memories from what Jung called the collective unconscious, but in this case, the memory triggered a spontaneous regression in me, the one assisting Val through her regression. Not a countertransference, but a totally complete past life recollection, I was placed in the middle of the scene as my colleague's regression was unfolding. A countertransference is when the therapist has an unconscious emotional involvement with the client, but this time, it was much more. It was an awakening of a traumatic memory that sent me into my own vivid story.

It stands to reason that souls have karmic ties resulting from incarnations of groups of people who come back together to resolve unfinished business as families, business partners, married couples, soldiers on the battlefield, and so on. In this case, two colleagues worked together to help each other move forward and refine their skills by alternating regressions to resolve complex issues. This allowed them to move toward uncovering the core archetypal patterns that would put an end to the cycle of karmic payback and paralysis in fear-based complexes.

As the client, Valerie had the impression of a young girl who came to her in a meditation just prior to the regression. Val knew that the girl held the key to some unresolved issue she wanted to investigate. The regression started with Valerie soliciting the girl to come forward. As she laid on the mat with her eyes closed, she could see the little girl's face. She was apparently very pretty, with long, curly dark brown hair and green eyes. Valerie saw her with her family somewhere in the country, living in a small cottage with her mother, father, and two siblings. She was about twelve years old, the eldest of the three siblings, she was helpful around the house, running errands helping her parents as best she could. She stayed close to home and didn't venture out much, so when her parents told her they were taking a trip into town, she was very excited. She was told to put on her finest clothes because they were going somewhere very special. The town they spoke of seemed to be Florence in the 1500s. The carriage ride appeared to take a long time, and they finally stopped in front of a large house surrounded by a high stone wall. As I prompted Valerie to go on, she described the house and what she saw inside. As she continued to describe the furnishings and layout of the parlor, I could see everything she was describing as if I were there in the room with her.

When the little girl and her parents went into the house, they were greeted by a man and woman who led them into a sitting room. A woman came out and gave the girl some grapes to entertain her while her parents went into an office with the owner of the grand house. The young girl, Clarissa, waited for a long time. Then the Madame of the house came back out and told the girl to follow her. Clarissa protested, demanding to be reunited with her parents, but she was told that they had gone and that they wouldn't be returning any time soon. When Clarissa heard this, she became hysterical and was taken upstairs to one of the bedrooms and locked inside for the rest of the night. She cried until she was exhausted and eventually fell asleep (shutdown moment).

The next day, two women came to her room: the Madame she first met when she arrived and another woman. They asked her to disrobe so they could get a good look at her. They then gave her some new clothes to wear. She was confused, scared, lonely. There were other young women in the house who came and introduced themselves to her and tried to make her feel comfortable. They seemed to make a fuss over her, fixing her hair and trying different outfits on her, but she felt awkward and wanted to be left alone. Then she met a young boy named Paolo. He was a little older but was very nice; she took a liking to him right away. He offered to show her around and told her about all his favorite hiding places. Paolo became her best friend. They played together all the time, but this diversion couldn't replace her longing for her mother. She still asked about her parents often and wanted to know when they would be coming back for her.

After a few weeks had passed, Madame came to her and told her there would be a special party in her honor. She was told to be on her best behavior and to look as pretty as she could because some very important rich people were coming to take a look at her. Clarissa still didn't understand what this was all about, but what was about to happen to her was going to change her life forever. Evidently, Clarissa's virginity was going to be auctioned off to the highest bidder when she was introduced to the social elite. She was to become the social highlight of the season and their new plaything. She was dressed in the finest clothes with perfume and makeup, paraded around the room for all to see and then positioned on a stage as the bidding began. When it was all over, one man came forward to collect his prize. He whisked her away to one of the upstairs boudoirs. She was petrified, with no clue as to what was about to happen. He tried to be gentle with her, but when he finally climbed on top of her, it hurt. It hurt so bad that she cried out, but he told her it was no use, he had bought and paid for her for the night and she now belonged to him. He hurt her again and again during the night until she was numb with pain and fear (another shutdown moment). He finally left her there in the dark when he was finished, cold and bleeding. She was too shocked to move and her legs were shaking so badly that when the girls came in to help her get up to wash, she couldn't move or speak. Her legs couldn't support her and she had to be carried to the bath.

The next day, she tried to walk down the stairs, but she couldn't, she hurt so badly. She started to cry. This time, Paolo came and said he would sit with her and tell her stories to help her forget. Clarissa now understood that Paolo must be suffering similar treatment. She felt sorry for him, but they never talked about it. It was like a truth they shared but didn't want it to interfere with their time together. When they were together, they could play and be children without a care in the world. As time went on, Clarissa was summoned by various men to perform sexual acts. She would climb the stairs and pretend to be someone else (dissociated). She became very good at pretending it was a game; she did what she had to do to survive, it was all very surreal to her. The only thing that was real to Clarissa was her playtime with Paolo. There, she could be herself. She trusted him and he was kind to her. They would play all day together until they were called in to work. Then they would pretend to be other people.

One day, several months after Clarissa arrived, a man came to the bordello. He was rich and very powerful, and he wanted Paolo. He spent the night with him, and by the time the morning came, Paolo was sick. This man had injured him somehow. He didn't feel right and he was bleeding. The Madame called the physician, but he couldn't stop the bleeding. He said Paolo had internal injuries and he could do nothing for him. Clarissa ran to him, holding on to him for dear life. Paolo never cried or complained, but within a few days, he slipped into unconsciousness and died. Clarissa was beside herself. She began to wander around as if in some kind of dream. She talked to Paolo as if he was still there, as if she had an invisible friend that only she could see (psychotic break). Nothing else seemed to matter. No one, not even her friend Rosa in the kitchen, could reach her. Rosa would call her to the kitchen and try to make special treats for her, talk to her, stroke her hand, and speak to her in a soft, low tone, but Clarissa didn't respond. She just stared into space. She was in her own world and no one could reach her.

Of course, she still had to work, but by this time she was so dissociated it didn't seem to matter. She went through the motions, but her mind was gone. She went through life as if her head wasn't attached to her body, like a plane set to autopilot. One day seemed to blur into another in an endless procession of sunrise to sunset. Only her memory of Paolo kept her alive.

Eventually, this beast of a man came back from his imposed scandalous exile. Everyone was afraid of him, and Madame warned him that he had to refrain from the use of excessive force. But she couldn't bar him since it was his kind that kept her in business. This time, he wanted Clarissa. She knew who he was and hated him for what he had done to Paolo. She wanted revenge. She plotted to kill him by bringing a knife into the bedchamber and hiding it under her pillow. She waited until he mounted her, then reached under her pillow and raised the knife up to stab him in the throat, but he caught her arm and made her drop it. He was so much stronger that she didn't have a chance. But he became so enraged that he grabbed her by the throat and strangled her. He went running out of the room, screaming, "The little whore tried to stab me! To think that she'd have the audacity to try such a stunt. Well, she'll not try it again, that's for sure!" He left, and all the girls came running, but of course it was too late. Clarissa was gone.

Now that she was dead, her spirit in the Bardo she could reflect on that life and her dying thoughts. Her final thought was "I don't want to do this anymore."

Rosa's Story

The interesting part about this regression was that Rosa was me, the therapist performing the regression. Rosa could see all the characters in the story and could feel the great fear and sense of helplessness that Clarissa felt. Rosa had been married to the Madame's brother. They were very happy for several years until he came to an untimely end by virtue of an accident. He was a tradesman who worked on the scaffolding, building part of the Palazzo Vecchio clock tower in the center of town. He fell and died as a result of his injuries. Unfortunately, young Rosa had no skills and no work or means of support. She seemed to have been alone in the world outside of her husband's family. After thinking over her situation, she decided to go to her sister-in-law to find work. She was welcomed into the bordello and given the position of headmistress. She had only one or two special clients and seemed to be at peace with this since in those days, if one wasn't married or living with a family, there were few jobs available.

As time went on, her one special patron was a man of great wealth and stature in Florentine society. He was very kind to her and showered her with gifts and special outings, during which she mingled with some of the prominent people of the day. Rosa became accustomed to this special treatment and thought she had won the favor of this gentleman. All was well until Rosa became pregnant. At that time, she thought her gentleman friend would welcome the bastard child into his life. She was so naïve and taken by his affections that she was totally mistaken. When he learned about the pregnancy, he became so enraged that he beat her and told her to never again think she could rise to his social level. The final straw was when he kicked her out of his room. He kicked her until she fell down the stairs. She broke her hip and lost the baby she was carrying in the process. She was laid up for quite some time and was afraid that she would wind up begging on the street since she couldn't work as a prostitute any longer. She again had to go to her sister-in-law and beg for some sort of work. This time, she put her to work in the kitchen preparing meals and doing laundry. This was where she met Clarissa and Paolo.

She was enamored with the two children since she didn't have any of her own so she mothered both of them. After the incident with Paolo, she went to the magistrate to ask for help out of fear for what might happen to Clarissa. They laughed at her and told her a common prostitute had no legal rights and they wouldn't bring charges against Madame because most of them were her clients. Rosa then went to the church, begging them to forgive her for her transgressions. Again, she learned that they had an allegiance to the Madame and were also clients of hers. Rosa became despondent and didn't know who else to turn to. Her worst fears were realized when the evil one returned to hurt Clarissa as she had feared. When she heard Clarissa's cries that night, she tried desperately to climb the stairs. But because of her broken hip, she was too late to help the young girl. She became despondent, like Clarissa had been after Paolo's death. Rosa attended the burial of the beautiful young girl but wanted to change the situation somehow. They laid Clarissa to rest next to Paolo in the garden behind the house. She went every day to pray for the pair, but she felt partly responsible for what had happened to them.

Eventually, she left the house and wondered aimlessly through the city streets until she found herself on a hill outside the city, looking down over the Duomo. She threw herself off the cliff onto the bluffs below, ending a tragic life filled with remorse and feelings of helplessness.

In the Bardo

In the Bardo, Rosa came to terms with the lover who abandoned her. She regained her sense of self by healing her broken hip and telling her lover that he was mistaken about her not being on his level. On the contrary, she was beyond reproach or social labeling. She became honorable in her ability to love unconditionally, having compassion for even the lowest of society's forgotten street urchins and whores. Her only regret was that she couldn't rescue Clarissa and Paolo from the entrapment of sex slavery. She tried in vain to rescue the two young innocents, but in the Bardo, she was reunited with the pair and was able to watch them grow up in a world that made no demands on them.

This regression was unprecedented in my experience, in that I knew this story so well and that it was part of my own past life memory. But I don't think it's out of the question to be connected to Val from a past life together. I know that certain people are drawn back together in different lives, in soul groups, to heal unfinished business from the past. When I first met Valerie at Dr. Woolger's workshop, we had the experience of having known each other before not ever having met before the workshop, it stands to reason that we had this past life connection and became fast friends. I believe my desire to help her in that lifetime led me to want to work with her in this lifetime. As far as Paolo is concerned, neither Val nor I have encountered anyone who meets the description of the young boy in the story. The man who threw Rosa down the stairs is a person I know well, who has a huge inflated ego, is from a very prominent Italian family, and still thinks himself to be very important. I have had several dealings with him and would not want to be associated with him on any level. It's common knowledge that the clergy and prominent heads of state in Rome and Florence participated in scandalous behavior in bordellos, using both young girls and boys for their illicit behavior. As a matter of record, the Bad Lorenzo of the de Medici family was one such individual, who not only participated in scandalous affairs but was also a murderer. It's hard to say who the evil man was in the story, but men with prominence and power can and do get away with the most heinous of crimes.

There are a lot of similarities between the stories of Shinwa and Rosa, and they seem to be lessons in self-preservation. Both women took their own lives. Both were without children, but not of their own choosing. Both became despondent because they had no control over the events in their lives. Shinwa could not forgive or forget what her sponsor did to her, not in that lifetime and not in the Bardo. She was dissociated because her sponsor tried to break her spirit. He tried to control her in every way. Trained as a geisha, Shinwa was used to strict discipline, but the training was teaching her an art form. That is very different from being made subservient to a controlling, power-hungry man.

Rosa also dealt with the difficulty of feeling like she had no one to turn to for help. She could deal with what happened to her, but she couldn't let go of what happened to the children. Feeling helpless is what drove her to the edge. The importance of balance between having control and being controlled is what we can learn from these lifetimes. Women have been fighting for their sovereignty for centuries. It is only now, in the twenty-first century, that women are finally being heard. Only now are their rights over their own bodies and rights to legal recourse being acknowledged.

Figure 10: Rosa, oil on canvas by G. C. De Pietro

Rosa and Shinwa both fought for their dignity and sense of self-worth. I think both women held on to who they were at the core of their being: loving and compassionate individuals who were not going to let anyone take their sense of self away from them. They knew in their hearts that if they stayed in their dire situations, their hearts would be broken, so they ended their physical and mental anguish.

A few years ago, I had a divination ceremony performed by a man named Glenn Leisching, who was trained in the South African shamanic school of divination. What he told me was very profound. He said that in this lifetime, I had to face the bully and end the drama once and for all. An ancestral lineage of women who were bullied has plagued me for many lifetimes. He went on to tell me that I had tried in earnest in two other lifetimes and didn't resolve it, but this time would be different. This time I would be victorious and end the cycle of abuse for myself, for my daughters, and for my daughters' daughters. I didn't know what he meant by all of this, but now, as I write this book and analyze these past lives, I think he was referring to Shinwa and Rosa.

They didn't have the support or the wherewithal to go the distance. A large part of the abusive culture is the elimination of the victim's support network. This ensures there is no one to turn to and the bully has the victim in a vise. But in this lifetime, things were different. Yes, I came from a family that suffered from domestic violence; my dad was a bully and practically destroyed my mom physically and mentally, but I learned from this. I went into therapy and then became a therapist myself. I understood how the system of degradation takes away a person's dignity piece by piece. I also learned that my dad's behavior was a learned experience that he was taught by his father, and so on. The problem was that all these women suffered in silence. They never told anyone about what they had to endure, and therefore they had no support network to call on. In these lifetimes, Shinwa wanted her friend to go the distance with her, but that didn't happen, and Rosa tried to get help, but her cries fell on deaf ears.

In today's world, you don't have to go it alone, and you shouldn't. You can hire an attorney or find and get family support. If you are in trouble and need help you can call the National Domestic Violence Hotline in the US at 1 800 799-7233. One in four women are victims of domestic violence. I know they can help you because I used to work for an agency here in the Hudson Valley that arranged for secure pick up locations that would take women and their children to undisclosed safe houses. They will offer you counseling services, a place to stay, and legal services. You are not alone. That's the lesson I learned: You don't have to do it alone. You can be strong and stand your ground, with loving and caring souls who have your back there with you in the battle. I don't think I could ever have thrown off the yoke of oppression if I hadn't done this regression work. I learned from all of my past lives that I've been down this road before, but that doesn't mean I can't change direction. We can turn right instead of left. We can climb higher and reach for the stars. I am not going to let my daughters follow the same path as their grandmother, aunt, and mother. It ends with me. As we continue our journey, you'll see how I managed to muster the courage to face the bully and win.

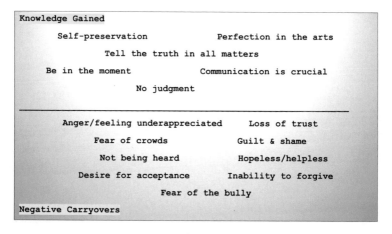

Knowledge Gained

Self-preservation   Perfection in the arts
            Tell the truth in all matters
Be in the moment   Communication is crucial
              No judgment

Anger/feeling underappreciated   Loss of trust
      Fear of crowds   Guilt & shame
      Not being heard   Hopeless/helpless
   Desire for acceptance   Inability to forgive
              Fear of the bully

Negative Carryovers

Chart 2

CHAPTER FIVE

THE ANCESTORS

After the divination ceremony with Glenn, I began to think very seriously about my ancestors and wanted to know where this whole story began. As part of my training, we delved into the possibility of inheriting karmas, phobias, thought patterns, and behavioral traits, and also dealt with general family patterns that resonated from one generation to another. I was beginning to think I had inherited a curse that was keeping me bound to an oppressive, male-dominated family structure.

Ancestral healing work deals directly with the spirits of generations past, helping them to release and heal their unfinished business and offers them the opportunity to find their rightful place in the afterlife so that present and future generations will be free from their lingering karmas and schemas. The reason a person is born into a certain family or ethnic group and lives in a certain place is not a random choice. Individuals are part of a deep web of interconnectivity that expands from their core through their families and all their relations, reaching to their communities and the collective world soul.

I understood that my family had a pattern of women being bullied and disrespected. I don't think Rosa and Shinwa were part of my family lineage, but I'm not certain. I submitted my DNA for testing and learned that I have 2 percent Asian DNA, 58 percent Greco-Roman, 11 percent Irish, 13 percent British, 11 percent from Europe and the Iberian Peninsula, and the last 5 percent is a mix of West Asia, the Caucasus, and Scandinavia. I don't believe that all past lives have to be part of a person's family line, but as a soul, it's possible to come back as one's own relative generation after generation. We learn from all of the cultures and ideals that our soul essence has experienced. This pattern of abuse has been evident in many of my lifetimes. It just happens to be a focal point in my life now and is one of the major reasons I have come into this life: to clear up.

In my DMP®, training I was taught how to draw a map of my family history as far back as I could remember. My mother's family never spoke to people from the outside world about anything personal. Not even to each other did they speak about matters of personal tragedy. As I look back, I remember my mother's father. He hardly ever spoke at all. It could have been partly because there was a language barrier, but even with his wife and children, there wasn't a lot of dialogue. I remembered being told that he had been a prisoner of war, held captive in the Alps during the First World War. He was eventually smuggled out and came to America around 1918. I think the poor man was shell-shocked. He never spoke about the war, so a hush fell over the family and no one ever talked about it. Even after my uncle died in the Second World War, no one ever talked about him. Only toward the end of my mother's life did she start to tell me about her brother, who died on Anzio Beach in Italy and was buried in my grandparents' Italian hometown in 1944.

My mother's mother, however, seemed to rule the roost because her husband didn't assume that role. But my father's father was a brute, a big man with a loud voice who made his presence known wherever he could. He was abusive to my grandmother and was a womanizer. My dad was abusive to my mom and very domineering. I needed to investigate where this all started in order to break the cycle.

In an ancestral regression, the facilitator opens and holds open the ancestral field so that a person's ancestors can speak through him or her and tell their story. In this regression, I acted as a channel for whomever needed to speak through me and clear the residue of the abusive pattern. It became abundantly clear during the regression that there has been an undercurrent running through all the women in my family of not being recognized for their talents, of being suppressed and dismissed and even abused. The women were continually put down and discouraged from going out into the world or being independent.

I needed to get to the bottom of it. I realized that I had to end this, not just for myself, but for all the women in my family. My mom was persecuted by my dad and he never encouraged or acknowledged her intellect or creativity. He discouraged her and put her down for things she wanted to do. I also think that deep down, he didn't trust her and thought she would be unfaithful to him. Given the fact that she was such a beautiful woman, he was insecure about their relationship, which led to power struggles.

Giovanni and Angelo, Italy, 1800's

During the regression, I found an ancestor on my father's side who came forward to tell me his story. This was a man whose wife was a stay-at-home mom. It felt like early to mid 1700s. Of course, women never went outside of the family for work in those days. Usually, they lived on a farm or had a family-run business to work on. This couple had one son and three daughters, and as the children grew older, the wife became restless. She wanted a creative outlet. This woman became friendly with the local baker, who was an older man, like a father figure to her. He offered to teach her the baking business since he could use an extra hand and she wanted to learn. The husband, of course, felt that it was more than that. He thought she had feelings for the baker and had lied to him about it.

He punished her severely and never let her leave the house without him. This woman did like the baker, but not in a romantic way. She found him to be a kind man who saw great potential in her and respected her for her talents. The husband was so jealous that he cursed this woman and her children's children. Of their three girls, two went on to lives of servitude, while the third dreamt of becoming a teacher but never achieved it.

The husband was so jealous and overreacted because of his history. We had to dig deeper into the story to find out why he felt so threatened. We'll call the husband Giovanni. As a child, he had endured the shame of coming from a broken family. He told us that when he was a child, his mother had a restless spirit. She fell in love with a traveling salesman who came through their town and eventually ran off with him, leaving Giovanni and his father to fend for themselves. She never came back and his father died of a broken heart. Giovanni never saw his mother again and was so hurt he never trusted another woman. He took all his anger and frustration out on his wife even though she was nothing like his mother.

We also learned that Giovanni's father, Angelo, was a very sullen man who couldn't or didn't know how to show his wife any love or affection. He was a working man who never had time for the simple pleasures in life. He was never able to express his emotions and died full of resentment toward the wife who left him.

In the Bardo

In the Bardo, Angelo was able to reconcile with his wife by taking responsibility for his own actions, which had caused his wife to leave him in the first place. He finally recognized that his wife had been starved for his affection, thus propelling her into the arms of the traveling salesman. Angelo's attitude toward his wife (mistrust and anger) was the model for his son Giovanni, who brought it into his own marriage. In the Bardo, Giovanni was able to see the truth: his anger created mistrust that clouded his mind. He was now able to see his wife for the innocent, talented woman she truly was. Asking her forgiveness was all that was needed for her to love him again and break the curse that he had sworn upon her.

Giovanni was also able to reconnect with his mother, who had abandoned him as a child. He found out that the salesman was unfaithful to her. She died alone and destitute, unable to find her way back to her husband because of her shame and because she couldn't forgive herself. Knowing she had paid a high price for the anguish she had caused softened Giovanni's heart. In the end, he was able to forgive her and welcome her back into the family.

This regression explains so much about mistrust and jealousy in my family. But, for some reason, I wasn't satisfied. I wanted to go deeper. I wanted to go back into my lineage and find a woman who was strong, one who was respected and looked up to in the family, someone I could derive strength from.

Tyrolean Couple, Austria, 1700s

In this regression, I had to go all the way back to Tyrolean times in Austria. Some say that these Tyrolean people descended from the Etruscans. The Tyrols came to prominence in the 1200s. I could see them in their costumes as they came forward. I got the feeling that the time period for this story was in the early 1700s. I was greeted by a woman in typical peasant costume.

Tyrol's as seen back in the 1700s. Typical dress of that time

Figure 11: Tyrolean Couple, google images.com

99

period, this family in my regression had a wool business in which the matriarch of the family was presumably a great-great-great grandmother of mine.

She seemed to be happy to meet me as she explained that they were a hardworking family. Theirs was a family-run business that seemed to deal with wool. They processed and sold the wool to others to make clothes. This woman, whose name I didn't hear (we'll call her Anna, my grandmother's name), was an integral part of the family business. Since the men in the family were mostly out in the field, she handled the arrangement of sales and also did the books. At times, she even had to go out to deliver the goods to different parts of the territory. She was smart and well respected in the family, a no-nonsense sort of person, but with a warm smile and big heart.

She was able to impart her strength to me and restore in me the respect that she was shown as an equal partner in all matters. She was a modern woman even though she lived centuries ago.

This story enables me to feel the positive aspects of a family partnership. My relatives in Italy are not too far from Austria in the Italian Alps. They have a prominent family business curing leather product, and the men and women all work together. These people are on my mother's side of the family, and it's interesting to me that they seem to have a lot in common with the Tyrolean family.

This next regression is not an ancestral regression, but more of a *shadow lifetime*: the kind of memory you would rather forget about because of the negativity and shame attached to it. However, it has a lot to do with my present-day family, as you will see in the people who play major roles in the story.

The Nanny, London, mid 1700s

The "Protestant Ascendancy" sought to ensure dominance by passing several laws to restrict the religious, political, and economic activities of Catholics and dissenters in Ireland. In the seventeenth and eighteenth centuries, Irish Catholics were prohibited by penal laws from purchasing or leasing land, voting, holding political office, living in or within five miles of a corporate town, obtaining education, entering a profession, and doing many other things necessary for a person to succeed and prosper in society. What was a person to do? The woman in our story had to leave Ireland in order to find work. She went to England, where Irish immigrants were welcomed as domestic helpers for the wealthy class.

This regression was prompted by the phrase, "I don't deserve to have anything."

The scene opened with a woman standing in a cold, dark place, being beaten by armed guards. She did not fight back, but rather accepted her punishment, saying, "I deserve this for what I did." We went back in the story line to find out what had happened.

This young woman, whom we'll call Ellie, was a nanny for a wealthy woman in London who lived in a large manor estate. Her Ladyship was married to a prominent lord in the House of Commons, and Ellie oversaw taking care of their only son, an infant. Ellie was an Irish immigrant who fled Ireland in search of work in the big city. She was a simple girl who worked hard and tried to do the right thing, but she never seemed to measure up to Her Ladyship. The noblewoman was hard on the girl, complaining that she was stupid saying, "Can't you do anything right?" and "Don't you know anything?" Day in and day out, Ellie found it harder and harder to stay focused because of the verbal abuse, but despite it, she tried to do her job. Ellie became especially upset when Her Ladyship said degrading things about the baby; she could take the harsh criticisms, but she couldn't stand it when her mistress came down on the baby. She would even tell Ellie to take the baby away from her because she said she didn't want to hear him cry or couldn't stand the sight of him.

Finally, Ellie reached the end of her rope and decided to do something really rash. No matter what happened, she wanted to protect the baby from this horrible woman. Ellie felt sorry for the baby and didn't want him to live a life without love. She couldn't stand the humiliation this woman inflicted upon her or her unloving attitude toward the baby, so she left the manor and took the baby with her. Ellie reasoned that Her Ladyship should have to pay for the way she had treated her and be made to reconcile the way she felt toward her baby. One night, while the lord and lady were out at a society function, Ellie bundled the baby up and took him to a cottage at the edge of the forest, outside the city. She had made arrangements to meet a friend at a certain place. Her friend had been trying desperately to have a baby and Ellie was going to give her this baby boy. In return, she would give Ellie enough money to book passage on a ship to America. When she arrived, however, her friend told her she didn't have the money. Ellie didn't know what she was going to do, but she couldn't go back to the manor. She tried to board a ship bound for America as a stowaway but got caught.

The authorities had been on the lookout for her since learning that His Lordship's son was missing. They questioned her and beat her but she wouldn't tell them what she had done with the baby. She was kept in prison until they arranged for a trial. While awaiting trial, she refused to eat and was ashamed of what she had done but would have done it again to protect the boy. Her friend came to visit her and told her she and her husband would do everything they could to make sure the baby was well cared for and they were sorry for not having the money to help her get away. Ellie didn't care anymore and was just waiting for it all to end. She didn't live long enough to face trial because she stopped eating and drinking. It didn't take long for her to pass over, and she was happy to die.

In the Bardo

Ellie didn't actually make it to the Bardo. Rather, she was left in a strange, dark place, not purgatory exactly, but a place like a void suspended between worlds, waiting there as if still on trial. The regression practitioner told Ellie that her ancestors were waiting for her in the Bardo. She instructed Ellie to look up toward the light, where they were calling for her. Ellie said, "No there is no one there for me, no family. I'm an orphan. There's no one waiting for me." Then she saw a hand reaching down into the void and a voice said, "Here, take my hand. I will pull you out." She took the hand and a handsome young man pulled her out. She thanked him but insisted she didn't deserve it. "Yes, you do," he said. "I have come to thank you for what you did for me. You saved my life and gave your own to give me a life of love rather than a life of misery. I had a wonderful family who loved me and helped me to open my own business. Thank you for your courage." It was the baby boy, now grown, who had matured into a fine gentleman. He had his own lumber yard, worked with his adoptive father, and was very successful and happy.

His parents also came to thank Ellie. Her friend said, "You paid a terrible price for what you did, and you don't need to suffer any longer. Come and join us in the light." Ellie hadn't thought anyone cared about her and now she cried, realizing that these people had cared about her and about what had happened to her. The practitioner asked me, as Ellie, about my biological family. What happened to them?

I told her my mother was a common prostitute who gave me up to the orphanage after I was born because she couldn't take care of me. She could barely take care of herself. She had gone to the city after the Irish famine of 1740, hit Ireland and tried to make a living. It was there, in the orphanage, that I met my friend, the woman I gave the boy to. She was my only friend and we both knew how horrible it was to grow up unloved. I couldn't bear to see that happen to the boy.

The boy's biological mother came to the Bardo to speak with Ellie. She said she felt no remorse for what happened to Ellie, and that she had gotten what she deserved. I told her that she had also gotten what she deserved: an empty house with no heir. "Why couldn't you give the boy one ounce of care or affection?" I asked. Her Ladyship answered, "I was forced into that loveless marriage because of my name. I hated it, and I hated my husband. I couldn't stand the sight of him, and the boy looked just like him, so I couldn't bare the sight of him either. I hated my life and I was jealous of you because you were free to be whoever you wanted to be. You were unencumbered by title and service. I yearned for the simple pleasures of life, so I tried to make you as miserable as I was."

The practitioner then asked whether anyone in Ellie's lineage could serve as an example of a strong woman with a sense of self-worth, someone who could stand her ground and was independent and happy with her place in the world. Ellie had to look hard, but a few generations back, she found a great-grandmother. She was a potato farmer in Ireland who worked the land and was happy with her place in the world. She knew that work was hard, but it was good, honest work. She had no self-doubt and did everything for her family to keep them together. She was proud of her family and took the bad times along with the good. When hard times hit, it was particularly hard on her family, but she was ready to wait it out. She knew it was only a matter of time before things would turn around. She never gave up. The daughters who left the farm were the ones who really fell on hard times. They lost their sense of purpose and pride, and little by little, they fell into poverty and shame.

This matriarch called all the women of the family together and told them that if they stuck together, they would wade through the hard times and support each other in the process. "Never give up, always stay together, and you will be strong," she said. Ellie found her family in the Bardo and knew she had finally made it home.

The boy in the story is my nephew now, who played an essential role in my emancipation from the bully in this life.

CHAPTER SIX

THE SHADOW

We all undoubtedly have a shadow side to our personality. Now, you could say that's our *id*, the term coined by Freud for one of the three subpersonalities he called the *id*, the *ego*, and the *superego*. The id is associated with instinctual drives, desires, and impulses. It represents the inborn, unconscious portion of the personality, where life and death instincts are responsible for human aggression and destructiveness, and possibly acts of heroism, in which an individual doesn't think about the consequences to his or her body.

This could also be a part of the sympathetic nervous system, which, when triggered by stressful events such as real or perceived life-and-death situations, releases hormones automatically in the body, causing us to react. This is often referred to as the fight-or-flight response. These functions are part of a system designed to keep us alive, which was particularly effective during prehistoric times when threats were sudden and sometimes unexpected; we had to act quickly in order to survive.

Adrenaline is released in times of danger, when we really can't afford to sit back and analyze the situation, we only have seconds to figure it out, and we can't wait. This has served us well; as you can see, there are billions of us on the planet. Having thrived here for millions of years.

In these regressions, we've seen id-like behavior, as in the young slave boy who stole and the nanny who impulsively took the baby without thinking of the consequences. How about the sailors who beat the Portuguese boy with the driftwood out of anger, not caring whether he lived or died, and the autistic boy who killed the baby because he had no filter to process what was happening to him?

These stories all exemplify human traits that we would rather not acknowledge in ourselves. You could even say they're barbaric, unfit for the civilized world, yet our impulsive nature is alive and well in the world today. Just scan the headlines in the evening news.

On a spiritual level, however, do these instinctual urges serve us? We will look at the shadow self as Jung wrote extensively about it: "We do not become enlightened by imagining figures of light, but by making the darkness conscious" (Jung, 1970, 220). As Dr. Woolger also wrote and taught, in the early stages of regression work, most people rarely get shadow figure memories, which are so violent. As a rule, the unconscious mind (which I now believe carries past life memories), only reveals memories that we are ready to deal with and able to integrate into our conscious personality structure (Woolger, 1988, 12).

It is here, however, in the shadow work, that we see our true nature, our essence. The shadow parts of ourselves are the polarized parts that we don't want to accept. When we go to the Bardo stage of the regression, we can gain perspective on the complex that Jung termed the *witness point* so we can see the mirror image. The murderer is murdered, the executioner is hung, and so on.

As I have shown in this research, we see in lifetime after lifetime that one life seems to balance out the other. This is difficult work, as St. John of the Cross said, "The dark night of the soul," describing the slow death and detachment from all lesser selves (Woolger, 1988, 329).

I consider the nanny a shadow personality. She didn't know love yet had enough compassion for an infant to do the unthinkable so he could have a life filled with love rather than a life like hers, which was void of love and in the end unbearable for her. It was only in the Bardo that she realized there were people who loved her and were grateful for what she did.

When this next story was first presented to me, I found it hard to assimilate; I was left trembling in fear and disbelief regarding the cruel nature of a man who was supposed to be holy, a man of the cloth. To get into the story, I was guided to visualize the shadow figure.

Figure 12: Monk, ink drawing by G. C. De Pietro

Father Amboise, southern France, 1230s

In a relaxed state, I asked this figure to come forward. I saw a hallway in an old cellar made of stone, like an old monastery. The stone walls were lit by torches fastened to the walls. I traveled along the hall until I came to wide stone steps going downward. I continued down the steps until I came to the bottom, into something like a crypt. I saw a monk standing there, an older man with white hair wearing a long brown robe tied at the waist with a thick cord. His name was Father Amboise. He said, "You have no idea how dark these days are, full of fear." During the Roman Catholic Inquisitions, the monks came under attack for harboring the ancient Gnostic texts that contradicted the church's teaching at that time. Gnosticism can be defined as follows:

> Gnosticism (from Ancient Greek: γνωστικός gnostikos, "having knowledge," from γνῶσις gnōsis, knowledge) is a modern name for a variety of ancient religious ideas and systems, originating in **Jewish-Christian** milieus in the first and second century AD. (wikipedia.com).

> Gnosticism says that humans are divine souls trapped in the ordinary physical (or material) world. They say the world was made by an imperfect spirit. The imperfect spirit is thought to be the same as the God of Abraham. Some **Gnostic** groups saw Jesus as sent by the Supreme Being to bring gnosis to the Earth (wikipedia.com).

This teaching went against the doctrine taught by the early church and was therefore forbidden. The Inquisition, set up in Languedoc by the Roman Catholic Church, seems to coincide with the information received in the regression pointing to the Medieval Inquisition. This Inquisition was established informally by Dominic under Pope Innocent III in the early thirteenth century. The express purpose of this original medieval Inquisition was to discover and eliminate vestiges of Cathar belief left in the wake of the Cathar Crusades.

We entered the scene with a monk hiding in the basement of the monastery, wringing his hands, not knowing what to do. "I am worried that the officials are coming for the manuscripts that the young monks were translating. I am worried that the monks will confess to hiding the texts and will be tortured for heresy. I don't trust them to keep the secret," he said. "I don't know what to do. There isn't much time. I hear the monks chanting their morning prayers. I must not let them be captured by the inquisitors. I am afraid they will tell them that the monastery has been translating the Gnostic texts. I have to protect the manuscripts."

Father Amboise found a torch in the hallway and threw it into the room where the monks were chanting, then bolted the door with a huge wooden beam. They couldn't get out. He heard them screaming as the room started to burn. "I can't listen to the screams. I must run to the chapel and prostrate myself on the floor before Christ and beg him for forgiveness for what I have done. I must grab my beads and pray. I will ask God to take the boys quickly so they will not suffer. Please forgive me for what I have done," he pleaded.

As Father Amboise, I knew I must hide the manuscripts. I ran through the monastery collecting all the books and buried them under the church. Hoping that they would be safe until a time when they could be brought out in a time of safety. I had to do this quickly because I knew they were coming. "Where can I go to hide?" I wondered. I smelled the smoke and saw the flames rising from the Abbey. The other brothers came, but it was too late. They couldn't be saved. The inquisitors came. They took me away. I was the one in charge, so they questioned me. "Who started the fire? Where are the novitiates? Weren't you in charge of them? What happened to them? What where you working on? Where are the books? Are they also in the fire?"

"You are lying," they said. "You must have the books. We want the books. Where are they? Take him away until he tells us where the books are." They took me to the dungeon and tied me up with my hands above my head and my feet barely touching the floor. They left me there for days and kept asking me where the books were.

> Tortures varied from time to time and place to place, but the following represent the more popular options. Victims were stripped and bound. The cords were tied around the body and limbs in such a way that they could

be tightened, by a windlass if necessary, until they acted like multiple tourniquets. By attaching the cords to a pulley, the victim could be hoisted off the ground for hours, then dropped. Whether the victim was pulled up short before the weight touched the floor, or allowed to fall to the floor, the pain was acute. This was the *torture of the pulley*, also known as *squassation* and the strappado. John Howard, the prison reformer, found this still in use in Rome in the second half of the eighteenth century (www.wikpedia.com).

"Please, I don't know," I begged. "Please give me some water." No water came. By the third day, I was delirious, forgetting everything. I couldn't think anymore. They beat me and asked again and again where the books were. I told them I would never tell them. I slipped into a coma. By the fifth day, I was dead.

In the Bardo

In the Bardo, I asked to see the young men who were under my care. They came in with their hoods up, chanting, surrounding me, singing louder and louder. I was their mentor. They looked up to me. I felt so guilty. I died thinking they would never forgive me, and God would never forgive me for committing such a heinous crime. I cried out for their forgiveness: "I am so sorry. I didn't want them to torture you. I only wanted to save the knowledge!" They came closer, still chanting. "Please forgive me!" Then they hugged me. They chanted my name, saying, "We died to protect the truth. We were doing God's work. We are martyrs for Christ."

I told them that I had never told the authorities where the books were, and they were safe. They were happy and patted me on the back. They said, "You did what you had to do. They would have killed us anyway, and they killed you too." I wanted to heal them. I called in the ancient healers to apply healing salve to their burns and asked for holy water for them to drink to clear out their lungs. The angels came and healed them and

me and gave us all healing water. We were so thirsty they c
let me drink any water, and the novitiates needed the wat_ ̲ʋ
clear the smoke from their throats and lungs. The angels also
applied steamed medicinal leaves to my wrists to heal my rope
burns from being tied up. It felt so good.

Next, I called in the magistrates. They stood and judged me
and again asked where I hid the books. I told them I was not
afraid of them anymore and there was nothing they could do
to me now. I was already dead, and I hid the holy books from
them because they would not have understood what those
books taught. Those books taught us that we were made in the
image of God and possessed the power of God. We didn't need
the church to reach God. They needed to know that the truth
was written in those books. The truth was that we are all kings
and their Church didn't want us to know that because they
would not be able to
control us if we knew
the truth. The Temple
of Wisdom had all the
knowledge, and they
could go there and
see for themselves.
They had been lied to
– fooled. They should
go to the Temple and
learn the truth once
and for all.

They were stunned
and whispered under
their breath. They
couldn't believe that
they had listened to
the lie for so long.
A team of angels
escorted them to the
Temple of Wisdom.

Figure 13: The Temple of Wisdom,
oil on canvas by G.C. DePietro

Then I called the king and church officials in to tell them they had forced people to believe a lie and they must now see and learn the truth for themselves. The king asked, "Who are you to tell me what to do? You are but a simple friar. What do you know? I am the king." I told him he must listen to the people if he wanted to be truly worthy to rule over them. If he knew the real truth, he would be a better ruler. He said, "I don't have to listen to you. You are just a peasant." But Jesus himself came and said, "You were king when you were on earth, but now you must abide by the rules of the heavens and the Universal Law, which is the absolute law – God's law, not man's law." The king bowed in front of Jesus and said, "I was doing what I thought the Church wanted; who was your representative on earth." Jesus replied, "Now you are in heaven and must learn the truth in all things. Go to the Temple of Wisdom and study the laws of the universe. You must learn humility and compassionate service to be a good ruler."

As a result, I, as Father Amboise, am finally cleansed of my guilt and feel that now the truth can come out. The world is ready to know the truth, and I don't have to live in fear any longer. My brothers have acknowledged me for my bravery and have forgiven me for their terrible fate.

This was a traumatic regression for me and left me shaking. I had a hard time owning what I had done to those innocent boys. I had spent a large part of my adult professional career working with boys because I felt compelled to do so. As an art therapist, I was able to reach many adolescent boys who were feeling hopeless, but I think they helped me more than I helped them. I don't know whether any of the boys I worked with in residential treatment were the novitiates in my monk story, but there was one boy who had burn scars on his hands and arms. It gives me chills even now when I think about it. I eventually wrote a book about my experience with those boys called *Abandoned*, but because of this past life, I had a very difficult time writing it.

I distinctly remember being paralyzed with fear when I sat down to write the book. I thought the authorities would find out about me and come after me. This, of course, was years before I did this regression. I even spoke to several colleagues about the irrational fear I had about writing that book. A few of them suggested it was probably an old story that I was still carrying around with me. Nonetheless, I put pen to paper and wrote it. Just before the book came out, the horrible feeling of being persecuted for my belief again overcame me. I pushed it out of my mind and finished the publication.

Now that I have experienced this regression, I understand where the fear came from. Hiding manuscripts and translating Gnostic texts in secret during one of the most contentious periods in Catholic history is an alarming reality to deal with. I have no idea where this abbey was, but the name I heard during the regression is of French origin and it may have taken place in the south of France. Many ancient writings about the Black Madonna (the Blessed Virgin Mary) and Mary Magdalene suggest that they left Jerusalem after Jesus was crucified, went through the south of France on the way to Glastonbury, England, in order to be safe. Several paintings and sculptures throughout southern France depict the Blessed Virgin with black or dark skin. Is it possible that there are some books hidden in an abbey there that include knowledge of what happened after Jesus died? It's an interesting thought, but I have no memory of where Father Amboise buried the books.

Thinking about the things I've learned thus far; I must admit that many of my lifetimes had to do with telling the truth or repairing the karma from telling a lie. In this last story, I am reminded of one of the biggest lies man has had to endure, that is, the lie the Catholic Church told us, that the only way to God was through the church. They reinforced it in our psyche through artwork, persecutions, wars, and crusades. The truth is that we are all made in the image and likeness of God. We don't need the church in order to reach salvation. We are one in the spirit, we came from the divine, and we will return to the divine. Sometimes I think the church has caused more war and division in the world than love.

If we understand that we evolve by the love we share, forgiving each other and seeing each other as brothers rather than separate beings, then we can truly begin to heal. This is the big truth that we need to remember: we are not separate from each other, and we are not separate from the divine.

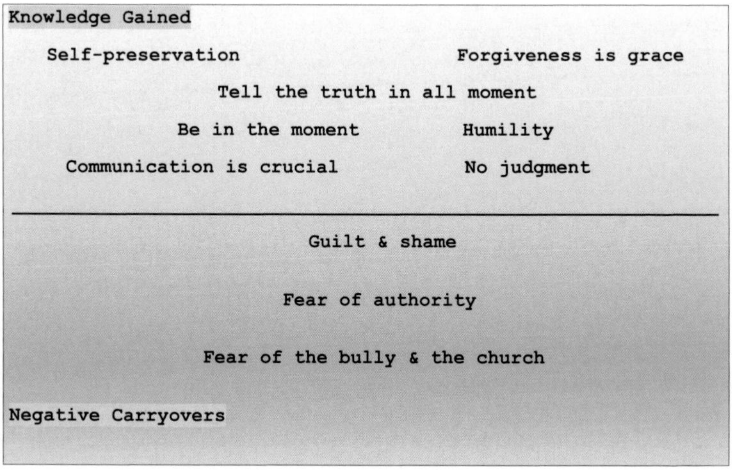

```
Knowledge Gained

   Self-preservation                    Forgiveness is grace
                  Tell the truth in all moment
          Be in the moment              Humility
      Communication is crucial          No judgment
_____

                     Guilt & shame

                   Fear of authority

             Fear of the bully & the church

Negative Carryovers
```

Chart 3

Professor Langdon, Cambridge, England, mid-1800s

Here is one more example of being intimidated for one's belief. Here we find a man who was educated, a researcher, and who thought outside the box. Again, it seems that his knowledge was too radical for the time he lived in.

What brought me into this regression was the phrase, "I'm not good enough," feeling like an outcast and misunderstood. The story began with the professor sitting on a bench in a railway station. He was confused and disoriented, not knowing where he was. He looked a bit disheveled and needed to be taken to the hospital. But this was the end of our story and we needed to go back to the beginning.

This esteemed professor, researcher, scientist, and lecturer, known as Professor Langdon, taught for many years at Cambridge in England. He worked very hard on his theory and was passionate about his teaching. His theory had to do with the electromagnetic pull of the earth by the sun, which was a fixed point in the universe connected to our earth's core. According to Langdon, this magnetic pull was enhanced by the crystals embedded in rock formations throughout the planet. He taught at the university for many years until he pushed his research too far and was dismissed because of it.

He spent the last ten years of his life trying to prove his theory, even spending his own money and traveling to Germany and other places to find people who might share his enthusiasm for his research. He became obsessed with proving the validity of his work and became destitute in the process. He eventually succumbed to alcoholism and died of a heart attack and sclerosis of the liver.

Figure 14: Euston Station, London, 1837 lithograph ©NRM Pictorial collection https://s3-eu-west-1.amazonaws.com/smgco-images/images/54/590/medium_1945_0052_0001.jpg

In the Bardo

The last few minutes of his life are cloudy because of his intoxication. It isn't until we get him detoxed in the Bardo that we can process what happened to him. In the Bardo, we find a young man in the railway station who found the professor. Evidently, this young man recognized the professor, which in the end was too much for him. The shame that he felt because of his failure caused the professor to doubt his abilities. He wanted to be anonymous so he could just become invisible and avoid the pain of being denigrated by his peers.

This young man went to the bench at Euston Station and said, "Hey mister, you can't sleep here. You have to move on."

Figure 15: Professor Langdon's Assistant, John, drawing by G. C. De Pietro

When the professor woke up, John, the train attendant, recognized him and asked, "Aren't you Professor Langdon?" He was so shocked to see the professor, a man he greatly admired, in such a state. John had been his assistant in the lab at the university. When the Professor was dismissed, his entire department was shut down. Causing John to go find other work, which was why he was working at the train depot.

The professor was totally shocked to see John. He didn't want anyone to see him in this condition, and he was mortified. While choking back his tears, he suddenly had a heart attack and died right there in the train station. John didn't know what to do. He couldn't believe the professor had fallen so far. He had such compassion for the man, whom he thought was brilliant. John stayed with him until the authorities came and went with him to the morgue until they could find his next of kin.

The professor had a sister who had also lost touch with him since he had become so despondent. John and the professor's sister made arrangements for his burial. She put a small notice in the local paper that the professor had passed and included the date of the burial service. As it turned out, scores of students came to pay their respects to the professor, as he was much admired by all the alumni. In the Bardo, the professor could see the turnout on his behalf and was greatly moved. It was there, in the Bardo, that he learned that he was ahead of his time. It wasn't that he wasn't good enough, but that his colleagues just couldn't grasp his concepts. He continued to grow in the Bardo by opening a school there for enlightened minds who could work on his theory. He was then able to call in the dean of the university to show him his work. The dean was still reluctant to change his opinion of the professor's work, but the learning continued and the dean was able to see the universe in a new way, to recognize that there was so much they still didn't understand about our relationship to the cosmos.

The professor was given a second chance to research and study the universe in a way he was never able to before. He realized that in his time, there just wasn't enough information available for the breadth and scope of what he wanted to do. Feelings of inadequacy were quickly washed away when the professor was able to continue his studies on the other side.

John and the professor were also reunited in the Bardo, where they decided to have a little fun by rafting down the rapids in the sacred river. This symbolized letting go of the fear of what other people thought of them. Water symbolizes allowing oneself to go with the flow without inhibitions and doubts. Now he knew he was good enough and could enjoy the process.

This regression seemed to amplify the misgivings I had about trying to get my first book published. Old feelings of being criticized and dismissed for radical ideas still tug at my psyche. That life was thwarted by the administration dismissing the professor for being too extreme. I can understand that the society in which he lived didn't expand its thinking to accept these kinds of ideas, but the sting of being ridiculed left a mark of doubt in my own abilities, which seems to carry over even into this life.

Then, of course, we had the subsequent lifetime of the mentally challenged life in which the young boy's mind needed a respite from being overstimulated with thought. This balancing of themes, feelings, and emotions seems to have been realized within these two lifetimes.

The Langdon story dealt head-on with the feeling of shame in a similar way to the monk in our last story. It wasn't until we got to the Bardo that we gained clarity regarding these two characters. Langdon had given in to his despair and stopped believing in himself. His confidence wasn't restored until he saw the students who turned out to pay their respects to him at his memorial. There, he realized that he had made a contribution and that he was respected. It is very humbling, in a way, to realize that you were loved by so many. The professor needed to acknowledge his own self-worth regardless of what others thought of him. Loving oneself in spite of limitations is key to understanding one's true identity.

This also brings to mind the need for authoritarian rule when it comes to those who think differently or oppose the status quo. We have seen this in several lifetimes in which the ruling class sought to punish and eradicate any opposing ideal or theory. This only proves that its power is based on a lie and maintained by ruling with an iron fist. We saw that in the

Russian story, in the political activist story, with King John in the debtor's prison story, and many others.

Given what I've experienced thus far, I feel that I have come into this lifetime again to do battle with the bully. I don't know where I got the strength to do this, since after all of my studies in psychology, I understand that long-term abuse causes people to believe they aren't good enough or deserve to be punished in some way. Women have been fighting this battle for eons, but it's not just women. It's anyone who may be different from whatever is deemed the norm. After centuries of being bullied, often a persecuted group will just give up. I don't think I would have been able to face the bully if I hadn't done the training in past life regression. I have come face-to-face with this trauma in so many lifetimes.

Tortured, killed, hung, mauled by a bear, beaten, jailed, scalped – the list goes on and on. These stories paint a dismal picture, but the Bardo work created a bridge for the physical, mental, and emotional bodies to heal. I've learned that I can forgive myself for the lies that I told and find the strength to tell the truth and that I don't have to do it alone.

The Dutch explorer learned to set sound boundaries, as did the Midwest girl. The Portuguese boy learned he was just as important as any other member of the crew. Natasha, the Nanny, Nancy, Adam, Shinwa and Rosa all had to stand up to the bully, if not in their lifetimes, in the Bardo. Learning self-respect seems to permeate all these lifetimes. We have collectively come a long way since the dark ages, when women were sold as mere property and had no legal rights or say in matters of state. But in this lifetime, I had to stand up to the bully in real time, as you will see in the parallel story of the Chinese girl.

The Chinese Girl (Third Century China)

The hook for getting into this story was the question, "Where did I first encounter the bully?" The importance of this question was that I had already dealt with the bully in many lifetimes.

I wanted to know where it all started. What was the situation that set the wheel in motion that then took so many lifetimes to unravel? I felt if I could uncover the first conflict, then the core belief structure would be transformed. We entered the scene with a ten-year-old girl bowing to the emperor. She was frightened because she was so young and because she was called from her home, where she had been secure with her parents, to the unknown world of the palace.

It appears she had been called to serve the royal family along with five other girls from her village that were about the same age. She was earmarked to be the handmaiden to the empress. It was supposed to be a great honor to be called into service, but our young girl was not happy at all to be separated from her family. She was required to go to a special school to learn how to bow and address the royals. She was also taught how to perform royal ceremonies and do other chores that were necessary for waiting on the empress. She was not allowed to talk to the other girls, as this school was very strict and did not permit any socializing. This girl, Jin, was very sad, deriving little joy from being in the palace. She was lonely, she missed her parents, never getting to see her family again. She longed for their companionship.

One of the first tasks Jin was asked to do was to carry water to the empress's suite using a long pole across her shoulders with a full bucket of water at each end. She was nervous but managed to carry the water a long way. However, in the process, she spilled some of the water on the floor of the entrance of the palace. She was brought before the emperor himself and reprimanded. He was a big man with a big voice and seemed to be intolerant of any mishaps. Jin was sent to one of the back rooms in the kitchen and made to kneel on bags of rice for several hours as punishment. Jin was even more despondent after this because she felt as if she couldn't do anything right and was being watched all the time. It was unnerving to her, but she carried on the best she could. Over time, she was summoned often by the empress, who seemed to take a liking to her. The empress was much nicer and kinder than the emperor, and Jin could see that even the empress had little influence over the emperor, who ruled with total control.

Time went on and Jin was given more and more responsibility. She was asked to run errands for the empress and on one of these occasions, she met a young man who worked in the stables. He took care of the animal's oxen, ducks, and chickens. He was very nice to her, one of the few people in the palace whom she could actually talk to. Over time, they developed a friendship. One day, the emperor saw her talking to this young man and sent him away to work in the fields. The emperor was a mean-spirited man who seemed to enjoy wielding his power over everyone. She was reprimanded and reminded never to talk to the young man again.

She didn't get the chance to see him often, but when she did, he told her how beautiful she was and that he absolutely adored her. She was so taken by this that all she could do was think of this boy and long to be with him. She snuck away as often as she could to see him and they started making plans to be together. They believed their only chance was to run away. One day, the empress gave Jin money to go to the market to purchase perfume for her. She ran straight to the fields, to her young man, and they took off running as fast as they could. They eventually arrived at a main road and caught a ride on a cart bound for the next town. They used the money to pay for the trip to take them as far away from the palace as possible.

Their victory was short-lived. They were caught when the emperor's guards stopped the cart and found them hiding in it. It didn't take long to bring them back to the palace. They were put in solitary confinement until the emperor could decide what to do with them. They were both sentenced to five years hard labor in the stone quarry. The young man cut the stone and Jin sorted it according to size and color. After several months of this work, she became very sick. It seemed as though the dust from the stone settled in her lungs and made her deathly ill.

She developed pneumonia, and a woman who worked in the quarry tried to heal her with teas and herbs, but it was no use. She died shortly after, at only sixteen years of age. As Jin, my final thought was only hatred for the emperor, which settled in my second chakra. This is what causes me weakness in the sense of who I am and how I project myself in the world. This set me up for lifetimes of abuse. My young man was by my side, crying that it was all his fault because he told me to run away with him. My body was placed on a funeral fire as the workers gathered to say their goodbyes.

In the Bardo

In the Bardo, the angels came to cleanse my lungs by having me drink holy water, then steaming the water for me to breathe in which penetrated deep into my lungs clearing out the pneumonia. I called in my young man, who told me how sorry he was for what happened. He adored me and would have done anything for me. He told me he never recovered from the loss. He spent ten years in that stone quarry, then eventually moved on. Back in the village, he married and had a family, but he never forgot me and never loved anyone else the way he had loved me.

The emperor was called in. I stood my ground and told him he couldn't intimidate me any longer. I also called in all my ancestors, who stood with me to face him. The emperor said I was chosen to serve him, it was an honor to serve him, and I disobeyed the rules. I went against the system of law and order. I disobeyed a direct order to not speak to that boy again. I opposed him and was punished for it. That is all. I countered that he had no compassion in his heart for anyone, he was feared by his people, not loved. Evidently, the Emperor was a lustful man and wanted all the pretty girls for himself. He did not tolerate any young man competing with him for the affections of an eligible young girl, especially one so pretty, and therefore he had to punish him.

We then called in the empress, who was loved by her people. She was a generous and kind woman, but she had no power and no say in how things were done in the palace. She had to endure a lot of humiliation due to the insatiable appetite of the emperor. I was sorry for deceiving her by taking her money. She was sorry that she couldn't help me and understood my desire to be this this young man wishing somehow things could have been different but she had no power to oppose her husband. Next, my power animal was called in to help me. Toucan squawked loudly. Toucan is called upon when one needs to be heard loud and clear, when it is important to make one's feelings, thoughts, and opinions known. This was the power that I needed to stop the cycle of abuse. I thanked Toucan for giving me this knowledge.

The emperor in that life was my business partner in this life. The empress in that life was my mother in this life. The young man in that life is someone I have yet to meet, but I will know him immediately when I do meet him by the intensity of his feelings for me and by his dark eyes. My business partner and I had a difficult relationship in this life. I was an equal partner in a business, a 50 percent shareholder. I had absolutely no say in what transpired in that arrangement since I was not the managing partner. In the beginning, it was set up with the caveat that there would be biannual meetings to review the budget for the year and oversee what expenditures would be made, but that never happened. I endured this subservient position in the company for fifteen years as I was legally bound by the partnership. When I asked to see the books, I was physically accosted and told to mind my own business. I was beside myself with frustration, I was forced to hire an attorney.

It wasn't until I had legal representation to get out of the partnership that things changed. Of course, my partner fought me all the way. He said the company would not function properly if it was split up. He told me he didn't want anyone looking over his shoulder telling him what to do. My feeling was that if I had no say in the day to day operations of the company then I didn't want to be part of it.

My family was there for me giving me the moral support I needed to see this through, I subpoenaed the books. My attorney was a very bright, successful lawyer; I also had the good fortune to have a family member take an interest in my case and offered to help me, he was a highly focused individual who spent hours poring over every detail in the books in order to find evidence of mismanagement. We found many discrepancies, sloppy bookkeeping, and inappropriate expenditures. It was a very long, arduous process that unfolded over the course of three and a half years. It tore me apart, but when I faltered, my family always encouraged me to go on. We dissolved the partnership and I was finally able to go my separate way. I have moved on. But it was a great sacrifice and at times frightening, since I had to face the bully and not succumb to his intimidation.

The young man who encouraged me and supported my efforts in this life was the baby in the nanny story I told earlier. I don't know if I could have gone through with it if it wasn't for his guidance, he was there for me in this life because I was there for him in the English lifetime. The empress was my mother interestingly, enough I could never figure out why her apartment was decorated in Chinese decor in this life. She had several Buddha statues, which was odd since we were raised Catholic. She had lacquered oriental style furniture with carved scenes of Chinese landscapes. After this regression, however, it made perfect sense. She always carried herself with grace and royal stature. She was admired by everyone who knew her, and she could very well have come from royalty as she exuded nothing less than perfection.

My business partner, I think, was Emperor Wu of the Jin dynasty. He became the first emperor of the Jin dynasty (265–420 AD) after forcing Cao Huan, last ruler of the state of Cao Wei, to abdicate to him. He reigned from 266 to 290, and after conquering the state of Eastern Wu in 280, was the emperor of a unified China. Emperor Wu was known for his extravagance and sensuality, especially after the unification of China; legend boasted of his incredible potency among ten thousand concubines (wikipedia.org).

Figure 16: Emperor Wu, Thirteen Emperors Scroll by Yan Li-pen
https://upload.wikimedia.org/wikipedia/commons/thumb/0/0d/
Jin_Wu_Di.jpg/220px-Jin_Wu_Di.jpg

In this life, he had a voracious appetite as well as extravagant taste. He is a big man who will boast of his great accomplishments. The emperor was a very powerful man and it seems as if it is difficult to be a common person after having such an experience, perhaps that is why he wanted absolute control in this life.

Facing one's greatest fear is not easy. At times, we just don't think we can. I learned that I didn't have to face it alone and I had to bolster my courage with whatever or whomever I needed to in order to get the job done. Sometimes, we just have to ask for help. In all honesty, it was a horrible experience, literally as contentious as getting a divorce. Looking back on all these lifetimes, it has occurred to me that I have been rehearsing for this day for a long time. The two biggest stories for me in all the regressions are the Japanese geisha girl, Shinwa, and the Renaissance woman, Rosa. These two women just couldn't overcome their abusive situations. Shinwa couldn't find the help she needed to fight and get her son back. What would have happened if she had confronted the couple who took her baby from her? It would have been a totally different story. And what about Rosa? She went to the authorities, but she couldn't find anyone to help her change the system, to protect Clarissa. What would have happened if she had taken Clarissa away with her to safety? Would she have been able to protect her?

I know that I speak about loving one another and being compassionate in order to live as one with respect for our brothers and sisters, for the planet, and for all living creatures. But that doesn't mean allowing someone to abuse you. It means setting sound boundaries and loving yourself enough to be strong in order to be there for those who do struggle. You can't do that if you're shaking in fear. If you must do battle, then fight to win. There is no shame in asking for help. I've gained awareness that my ex-business partner came to fulfill a contract that was planned a long time ago in order for me to accomplish the goal of standing up to the bully. That realization only came to me after the battle had been won. I still had to go through it; I had to speak up, to find my voice, to let go of my hatred long enough to achieve a clear objective. I appreciate it now, for what it's worth, to be able to move forward with confidence. I was able to fight the good fight and win. I know now that I could do it again if I had to – not that I want to. I think once is enough! Once bullies are confronted, they aren't so scary anymore. They are usually full of hot air and as frightened as you are. They just have a better defense mechanism.

What I have learned Overall
Self-preservation Forgiveness is grace Love yourself
Tell the truth in all matters   Be in the moment
Humility
Authority figures aren't always right
Communication is crucial   No Judgment
Don't let anyone bully you
What I'm still working on
Speak up when you need to   Don't be afraid
Surround yourself with those
who love you and who are there
for you

Chart 4

I have seen people transform by doing this work, such as women who were sexually abused as children, who were so afraid to be seen or heard that they cowered in the darkness. Once they found the courage to do this work, they became stronger with each layer that was peeled away. It's not easy work, as you can see by the harrowing stories that I've presented here in this exposé. If an individual can take the first step toward reclaiming his or her power, it will be possible to shake off the fear that keeps you chained.

CHAPTER SEVEN

THE ULTIMATE GOAL

R emembering the past is a formidable task for anyone. It is not, however, the ultimate goal to remember all of our past lives, only the ones that are still influencing your present-day reality. Reliving our past lives can cause us to reassess who we thought we were. It has become evident to me that our higher self will only allow us to process the lifetimes that are pertinent to us now and the ones we can emotionally handle. After we've lived so many lifetimes, many of our complexes have been resolved and we have moved on from them. There doesn't seem to be a need to review them again. If we have processed all that we need to, then what's next? Is there more to be experienced?

In my research, it seems as if we go through major cycles in our evolutionary process. According to many ancient books, such as the Bible, the Qur'an, the Book of Enoch, the Vedic texts, and the Hindu and Zoroastrian scriptures, just about every major religion on earth foretells of an event that occurs at the end of an age called the solar flash, which comes at the end of a cycle. An age is a cycle of 25,920 years. When each cycle ends, there is a **"harvest"** a term used in the Bible and in *The Law of One*, meaning essentially the evolution of souls from a third density to a fourth density being or **"light body."** We have three chances to move out of the third density realm which is what we are in now. These three cycles give us a chance to evolve to a fourth density which concludes in a harvest. If, at the end of the third cycle, we still haven't learned our core lessons, we will have to move to another third density planet to start the 25,000-year cycle all over again. (Wilcock, *Wisdom Teachings*, Nov. 6, 2017 S/27, Ep.13, www.GaiaTV.com).

The process here is that as we clear out old karmic patterns, we become more enlightened, hopefully, to the extent that we no longer have to incarnate. As long as this occurs, we've learned our lessons and cease to create more negative karma for ourselves. Any unresolved negative thought patterns in our reality will continue to seek out a life form in order to work out the complex. Every thought and action need to be carefully guarded to avoid creating more negativity. I do believe that is why some choose to sit in meditation and pray; in order to stop the cycle. In *The Law of One* readings, it says that forgiveness stops the wheel of karma. Forgiveness, acceptance, and love are required in order to stop the cycle and acquire a light body.

Light Body and Ascension

The concept of a light body has been discussed since the beginning of time. Very few people have achieved this, but it is documented that through the ages over 100,000 people in Tibet and China have done this through meditation, contemplation and forgiveness. They were able to transform a physical body into a light body, or what some refer to as a rainbow body. As Jesus of Nazareth did when he rose from the dead.

I venture to say that this is the end game for each soul to achieve. After living thousands of lifetimes, we can eventually reach the state of being described in the holy books. You may think this is impossible but in *The Law of One* it states that we need only be 51 percent positive, kind, loving, and compassionate. Not only do humans undergo this transformation, but the earth itself goes through a density shift and becomes a fourth density planet, what the Bible describes as the creation of a new heaven on earth.

According to *The Law of One,* we are at the end of an age in which not only do we evolve, but the planet does as well.

First density corresponds to the root chakra, represented by the color red, which is located at the base of the spine in physical human manifestations on the earth plane. First density is also the formation of minerals, earth, air, fire, and water, on the planet, known as the elements. Second density corresponds to the sacral chakra, manifested as the color orange in the space above the pubic bone in the human body. The earth's evolution to the second density is single-cell organisms, plants, fish, birds, and mammals. Third density corresponds to the solar plexus or the gut, represented by the color yellow. The earth's evolution in third density is self-awareness, as in human consciousness, the id, the ego, and the super ego. Fourth density is the heart chakra, represented by the color green, manifesting as love of others and service to mankind. (Wilcock, *Wisdom Teachings*, March 2016, S20 Ep.5 www.GaiaTV.com). This is the juncture we are in right now. We cannot move into the heart chakra while still harboring hate, resentment, deceit, loathing, or any of the lower emotional states of the third density. This is the main purpose of clearing up our karma, to move into the higher states of consciousness. The best way to do this is to be of service, to be caring and loving to our fellow man. Animalistic behavior is not permitted in the fourth density. At the end of the third cycle, we have a chance to ascend to a fourth density or light body. In many holy books this is referred to as the harvest.

According to *The Law of One*, the harvest cycle is as follows:

Book One, Session 14: 14-15

1) It is however, more toward the median or mean, shall we say of third-density developments throughout the one infinite universe that there be a small harvest after the first cycle.

2) The remainder having significantly polarized, the second cycle having a much larger harvest.

3). The remainder being even more significantly polarized, the third cycle culminating the process and the harvest being completed. (Wilcock, *Wisdom Teachings*, March 2018, S20 Ep.5 www.GaiaTV.com).

It seems to me that at this time, we are more polarized than ever before, not just in the US but all over the world. Families are torn apart by political ideologies, by religious beliefs, and by social economic standings.

The following is found in *The Law of One,* Book Three, quote. Session 63:9:

Question:

Now, at the present we have, in third density incarnations on this plane those third density entities of the planet earth who have been here for some number of incarnations who will graduate in the three-way split.

Response:

Either positive polarity remaining on earth for fourth density experience on the plane. The negative polarity harvestable gong to another planet. Or they are not harvestable and have to move to another third density planet or the positive oriented harvested entity will remain on this planetary influence but not upon this plane. (Wilcock, *Wisdom Teachings*, March 2016, S20 Ep.5 www.GaiaTV.com).

This means there will be those of harvestable nature who will go on to a fourth-density planet. Some will be at a fourth-density level but remain on this planet in another plane of existence, and some who are still too negative to be harvested will have to remain and repeat the cycle on a third-density planet (if not Earth than another similar planet).

The Law of One, Book One, Session 6:13 reads:

Question: What is the length, in our years, of one of these cycles?

Answer: One major cycle is approximately 25,000 of your years. There are three cycles of this nature during which those who have progressed may be harvested at the end of three major cycles. That is, approximately between 75,000 and 76,000 of your years. All are harvested regardless of their progress, for during that time the planet itself has moved through the useful part of that dimension and begins to cease being useful for the lower levels of vibration within that density.

The Law of One, Book One, Session 14:15

Explains that at the end of our first cycle, no one was harvested. This means there was not one person who could advance to a fourth-density level. Then it states that at the end of the second cycle, the harvest was extremely small. There were some however, who could have advanced to a fourth-density level but chose to stay to help others achieve a harvestable level (Wilcock, *Wisdom Teachings,* March 2016, S20 Ep.5 www.GaiaTV. com).

There seems to be a very negative force here on this planet that keeps us in a war-like mentality in order to preserve us as a slave race for the elite. It is up to each one of us to wake up. At this time, I believe a great polarization is occurring that is forcing us to choose a side. We are either positive or negative in service to others, loving and caring, or we are self-absorbed, consumed with greed and power. It is time to choose one side of the fence or the other; we can't straddle the fence. Polarization helps to make this very clear. We are either good or evil positive or negative. There is no in-between. Again, in *The Law of One,* it states you only have to be 51 percent in service.

All of the following Bible references are taken from the King James Version in I Corinthians 15: 45–53 it says:

45 And so it is written, The first-man Adam was made★ a living soul; the last Adam was made a quickening spirit

46 Howbeit that was not first which is spiritual, but that which is natural; and afterward that which is spiritual.

47 The first man is of the earth, earthy: the second man is the Lord from heaven.

48 As is the earthy, such are they also that are earthy: and as is the heavenly, such are they also that are heavenly.

49 And as we have borne the image of the earthy, we shall also bear the image of the heavenly.

50 Now this I say, brethren, that flesh and blood cannot★ inherit the kingdom of God; neither doth corruption inherit incorruption.

51 Behold, I shew you a mystery; We shall not all★ sleep, but we shall all be changed,

52 In a moment, in the twinkling of an eye, at the last trump: for the trumpet shall sound, and the dead shall be raised incorruptible, and we shall be changed

53 For this corruptible must put on incorruption, and this mortal must put on immortality. (Wilcock, *Wisdom Teachings*, March 2014, S8 Ep.1 www.GaiaTV.com).

If a mortal man can't enter the kingdom of heaven as a physical being, then it stands to reason that he will have to take on a light body, moving from a third density to a fourth-density. This will happen in the last moment (the solar flash), at the last trumpet (sound vibration), in the twinkling of an eye.

Matthew 13:24–30 relates Jesus's words about "the harvest":

24 Another parable put he forth unto them, saying, The kingdom of heaven is likened unto a man which sowed good seed in his field:

25 But while men slept, his enemy came and sowed tares among the wheat, and went his way

26 But when the blade was sprung up, and brought forth fruit, then appeared the tares also

27 So the servants of the householder came and said unto him, Sir, didst not thou sow good seed in thy field? from whence then hath it tares?

28 He said unto them, An enemy hath done this★. The servants said unto him, Wilt thou then that we go and gather them up?

29 But he said, Nay; lest while ye gather up the tares, ye root up also the wheat with them.

30 Let both grow together until the harvest: and in the time of harvest. I will say to the reapers, Gather ye together first the tares, and bind them in bundles to burn them: but gather the wheat into my barn (Wilcock, *Wisdom Teachings*, Nov.6 2014, S27 Ep.13 www.GaiaTV.com).

The barn is the safe place where he will take the righteous and good. Jesus says to let the weeds grow alongside the wheat until the harvest. I believe this is the end of days or the end of the third major cycle of 75,000 to 76,000 years. At that time, he will gather the tares and burn them. I believe the tares are the wicked, greedy who rule this planet and try to hold us down by using negative fear tactics.

Matthew 13: 31-41 shares more about "the harvest":

31 Another parable put he forth unto them, saying, The kingdom of heaven is like to a grain of mustard seed, which a man took, and sowed in his field:

32 Which indeed is the least of all seeds: but when it is grown, it is the greatest among herbs, and becometh a tree, so that the birds of the air come and lodge in the branches thereof.

33 Another parable spake he unto them; The kingdom of heaven is like unto leaven, which a woman took, and hid in three measures of meal, till the whole was leavened

34 All these things spake Jesus unto the multitude in parables; and without a parable spake he not unto them:

35 That it might be fulfilled which was spoken by the prophet, saying, I will open my mouth in parables; I will utter things which have been kept secret from the foundation of the world

36 Then Jesus sent the multitude away, and went into the house: and his disciples came unto him, saying, Declare unto us the parable of the tares of the field

37 He answered and said unto them, He that soweth the good seed is the Son of man;

38 The field is the world★; the good seed are★ the children of the kingdom; but the tares are the children of the wicked one;

39 The enemy that sowed them is the devil★; **the harvest is the end of the world; and the reapers are the angels**

40 As therefore the tares are gathered and burned in the fire; so shall it be in the end of this world.

41 The Son of man shall send forth his angels, and they shall gather out of his kingdom all things that offend, and them which do iniquity; (Wilcock, *Wisdom Teachings*, Nov.6 2014, S27 Ep.13 www.GaiaTV.com).

The Law of One authors refer to the souls as being harvested just as it is stated here. As for the angels, I believe they are light beings in the astral realm who will return to get us. As it says here, the reapers are the angels.

Matthew 13: 42–44 offer further detail about "the harvest":

42 And shall cast them into a furnace of fire: there shall bewailing and gnashing of teeth

43 Then shall the righteous shine forth as the sun in the kingdom of their Father. Who hath ears to hear, let him hear

44 Again, the kingdom of heaven is like unto treasure hid in a field; the which when a man hath found, he hideth, and for joy there of goeth and selleth all that he hath, and buyeth that field (Wilcock, *Wisdom Teachings*, Nov.6 2014, S27 Ep.13 www.GaiaTV.com).

This knowledge is like a precious treasure that has been hidden, but those who hear it are the blessed ones. In verse 43, it says the righteous will shine forth like the sun. I believe this refers to the taking on of a light body, as Jesus did when he rose from the dead.

In 2 Peter 3:13–14, we learn that:

13 Nevertheless we, according to his promise, be for new heavens
and a new earth, wherein★ dwelleth righteousness

14 Wherefore, beloved, seeing that ye look for such things, be diligent that ye may be found of him in peace, without spot, and blameless

Without Spot…they mean caring, loving… with no malice in their hearts. (Wilcock, *Wisdom Teachings*, March 2014, S8 Ep.1 www.GaiaTV.com).

According to Isaiah 65:17:

> **17** For, behold, I create new heavens and a new earth: and the former shall not be remembered, nor come into mind

According to Isaiah 66:22:

> **22** For as the new heavens and the new earth, which I will make, shall remain before me, saith the LORD, so shall your seed and your name remain

Your essence of who you are, your DNA shall not change. (Wilcock, Wisdom Teachings, March 2014, S8 Ep.1 www. GaiaTV.com).

Luke 21: 25-28 says

> **25** And there shall be signs in the sun, and in the moon, and in the stars; and upon the earth distress of nation, with perplexity; the sea and the waves roaring;

> **26** Men's hearts failing them for fear, and for looking after those things which are coming on the earth: for the powers of heaven shall be shaken.

> **27** And then shall they see the Son of man coming in a cloud with power and great glory

> **28** And when these things begin to come to pass, then look up, and lift up your heads; for your Redemption draweth nigh. (Wilcock, *Wisdom Teachings*, March 2014, S8 Ep.1 www.GaiaTV.com).

The signs in the heavens can be interpreted as astrological signs of an imminent event, such as in a pole shift or solar flash. Then the Son of Man will come in a cloud he is a celestial being returning as predicted. In the Book of Enoch, an example of this prophecy comes to us from ancient, times reiterating that the harvest, the polar shift, and the solar flash as we now think of it are at the end of an age or cycle.

Enoch was Noah's grandfather. He wrote his prophecies down, but they weren't discovered until 1773 by Scottish explorer James Bruce in Ethiopia. Dr. Richard Lawrence translated the texts in 1821. Jesus himself quoted from Enoch who was in direct contact with those entities known as the Elohim, which in the Hebrew Bible are Gods. (Wilcock, *Wisdom Teachings*, Sept.25, 2017 S27 Ep.7 www.GaiaTV.com).

According to Enoch I: 1–3:

1   The words of the Blessing of Enoch, where with he blessed the elect and righteous, who will be

2   living in the day of tribulation, when all the wicked and godless are to be removed. (Those who defile the earth now). And he took up his parable and said: Enoch, a righteous man whose eyes were opened by God saw the vision of the Holy One in the Heavens which the Angels showed me

3   And from them understood as I saw It was not for this generation but for a remote one which is yet to come (Wilcock, *Wisdom Teachings*, Sept.25, 2017 S27 Ep.7 www.GaiaTV.com).

Enoch 80:2 says:

And in the days of the sinners the years shall be shortened

And their seed shall be tardy on their lands and fields

And all things on the earth shall alter

And shall not appear in their time

And the rain will be kept back. *(Earth Changes)* (Wilcock, *Wisdom Teachings*, Sept.25, 2017 S27 Ep.7 www.GaiaTV. com).

Enoch 1:5-6

5   And in those times the fruits of the earth shall be
       backward.
       And shall not grow in their time
       And the fruits of the trees shall be withheld in
       their time
       And the moon shall alter her order
       And not appear at her time. *(Polar Shift)* (Wilcock,
       Wisdom Teachings, Sept.25,2017 S27 Ep.7 www.
       GaiaTV.com).
       And in those days the sun shall be seen and he shall
       journey in the evening on the extremity of the
       great chariot in the west.
       And shall shine more brightly than accords with
       the order of light. *(Solar Flash)*

6   And many chiefs of the stars shall transgress the
       order prescribed
       And these shall alter their orbits and tasks
       And not appear at the seasons prescribed to them.
       And the whole order of the stars shall be concealed
       from the sinners and the thoughts of those on the
       earth shall err concerning them
       And they shall be altered from all their ways
       Yea they shall err and take them to be Gods.
       The greedy ruing class will not see the changes
       coming because of their arrogance. (Wilcock,
       Wisdom Teachings, Sept.25, 2017 S27 Ep.7 www.
       GaiaTV.com).

1:3-8

3   The Holy Great One will come forth from his
       dwelling

4   And the eternal God will tread upon the earth
       even on Mont Sinai

And appear in the strength of his might from the heaven of heavens

5   And all shall be smitten with fear
And the watchers shall quake, holies will come down

6   And the high mountains shall be shaken
And the high hills shall be made low
And shall melt like wax before the flame

7   And the earth shall be wholly rent in sunder
And all that is upon the earth shall perish
And there shall be a judgement upon all men

8   But with the righteous. He will make peace
And will protect the elect
And mercy shall be upon them
And they shall all belong to God,
And they shall all be blessed
And He will help them all
And light shall appear unto them
And He will make peace with them. (Wilcock, *Wisdom Teachings*, Sept.25, 2017 S27 Ep.7 www.GaiaTV.com).

Enoch 45:3-6 says:

3   And their souls shall grow strong within them when they see Mine Elect Ones.
And those who have called up my glorious name:

4   Then will I cause Mine Elect One to dwell among them
And I will transform the heaven and make it an eternal blessing and light.

5   And I will transform the earth and make it a blessing

And I will cause Mine Elect Ones to dwell upon it:
But the sinners and evil doers shall not set foot there on.

6   For I have provided and satisfied with peace My righteous ones
And have cause them to dwell before me
But for the sinners there is judgement impending with me
So that I shall destroy them from the face of the earth. (Wilcock, *Wisdom Teachings*, Sept.25,2017 S27 Ep.7 www.GaiaTV.com).

This seems to be very reminiscent of the Book of Revelations in the Bible. I believe it is describing the end of an age, when a shift takes place a solar flash and pole shift in which the earth is destroyed and with it all those who are evil. But those who have open hearts, who are loving and kind, will be brought up to the light. "Mine Elect Ones" might refer to angelic beings or those who are already in light bodies who will again come and live on earth.

Excerpts from the Qur'an in a book entitled *Heart of the Qur'an* "Meditations on the Holy Qur'an Day of Atonement", p. 71 tells us that:

When time suddenly disappears, in the eternal moment of illumination the brightness of the heavenly orbs will be split open and dissolved into transparent light... Those who fail to live in constant expectation of the Mystic Day regarding this teaching as myth or imagination, will be severely disappointed when the Last Day actually arrives and they are not spiritually prepared. ("Meditation on Holy Qur'an", 77:8, 15) as taken from David Wilcock, *The Ascension Mysteries*, p 269. (Wilcock, *Wisdom Teachings*, Nov.13,2017 S27 Ep.14 www.GaiaTV.com).

The orbs will be split open as in a solar flash. Time comes to an end as stated in I Corinthians 52:52:

> In a moment, in the twinkling of an eye, at the last trump:
> for the trumpet shall sound, and the dead shall be raised
> incorruptible, and we shall be changed
> As noted from p. 195

And in Peter 2:13:

> Nevertheless we, according to his promise, look for
> new heavens and a new earth, wherein★ dwelleth
> righteousness (Wilcock, *Wisdom Teachings*, Nov.13, 2017
> S27 Ep.14 www.GaiaTV.com).

According to "Meditation on the Holy Qur'an" 76: 6-13, The Day of Truth:

> Upon the mysterious Day when time ends
> All manifest being will tremble at the first thundering
> blast of Divine Resonance that will utterly stop the world.
> (Taken from Wilcock, *The Ascension Mysteries,* p 269).

If the rotation of the earth were to stop as in a recalibration of a polar shift, this momentary terror would disappear when each soul realizes its spiritual body to be perfect, limitless and holy. (Wilcock, Wisdom Teachings, Nov.13, 2017 S27 Ep.14 www. GaiaTV.com).

According to "Meditation on the Holy Qur'an" 88:1-5, Day of Truth:

> You must come to know with absolute certitude
> That from above your conscious being, as stars above
> The earth, there gaze angelic protectors. Upon pages of
> light in the invisible book of your life which will become
> visible on the Day of Truth. These heavenly beings record
> all your actions and reactions. Even the most secret
> motivations they perceive and transcribe with perfect

clarity. (Wilcock, *Wisdom Teachings*, Nov.13, 2017 S27 Ep.14 www.GaiaTV.com).

According to "Meditation on the Holy Qur'an" 82: 10-12, Day of Enlightenment:

> When the Day of Enlightenment dawns, the soul
> Expressed as a luminous body, the face of its being
> Suffused with calm joy. Awakens into the supernal garden
> of Divine Presence, overwhelmed to comprehend at last
> the full. Significance of its own spiritual commitment.
> (Wilcock, *Wisdom Teachings*, Nov.13, 2017 S27 Ep.14
> www.GaiaTV.com).

It seems very clear to me that the soul works to become a fully realized spiritual being.

According to "Meditation on the Holy Qur'an" 99:4, Resurrection, we see that:

> On that timeless and transcendent Day human beings
> Will experience resurrection in bodies composed of
> Light. And we will be shown clearly all the thoughts and
> Actions of their lifetimes. (Wilcock, *Wisdom Teachings*,
> Nov.13, 2017 S27 Ep.14 www.GaiaTV.com).

"Meditations on the Holy Qur'an" 42:7, Day of Clarification says:

> How few human beings understand the intensity and
> Magnitude of the swiftly approaching Day of
> Clarification. Those who do not really comprehend the
> nature of the Last Day are impatient and would like to
> speed its arrival, whereas those who know the immense
> power of the Living Truth. Stand in trembling awe
> Before the dawning of this infinite Day. (Wilcock, *Wisdom
> Teachings*, Nov.13, 2017 S27 Ep.14 www.GaiaTV.com).

Clearly, this day will come, and I believe it will happen in my lifetime; therefore, it is time to get ready.

"Meditations on the Holy Qur'an 5:51", All Faiths says:

If each spiritual nation practices faithfully the path
Revealed through its own Holy Prophets. Then all
humanity will return together to the Source of Love.
(Wilcock, *Wisdom Teachings*, Nov.13, 2017 S27 Ep.14
www.GaiaTV.com).

I love this quote because it says we can all attain spiritual enlightenment, whether we are Muslims or Jews, Christians or Buddhists. We can all reach illumination.

In *Buddhist Prophecies: The Buddhist Conception of Time and Temporality* by David J. Kalupahana,

Vol 24, No 2, Time and Temporality (April 1974, University of Hawaii Press, pp. 181–191), we learn about the

Hindu concept of time:
The Hindu word for time is Kala
It is looked at as not only the cause of
The universe but an all-pervading principle
That governs everything in it
The Jains and others later saw time as one
Of the causes that determine the course of
Natural phenomena. (Wilcock, *Wisdom Teachings*, Nov.20,
2017 S27 Ep.15 www.GaiaTV.com).

This means that growth takes time to develop. Now, let's examine the Buddhist concept of time:

Buddha realized that everything is causally
produced – by time

Everything in this world is impermanent.
Buddha also believed the beginning of the
Universe was inconceivable Anamattagga.
Despite an inconceivable beginning, we

Witness periods of evolution – vivatta
and dissolution – samvatta.

The periods of vivatta and samvatta play out in terms of aeons.

In Buddhist terms these aeons are called Kappa
The Buddhist term "Samvatta" appears to be
Directly based on the Hindu samvartaka.

The Hindus believe that the samvartaka fire occurs at the end
of an age.

The largest Kappa in Buddhism is the Maha-
Kappa (or 25,920-year cycle)
A Kappa is the end of a cycle
The ending of a Maha-Kappa produces an
Apocalypse that can happen in three ways
Water, Fire and wind. (Wilcock, *Wisdom Teachings*,
Nov.20, 2017 S27 Ep.15 www.GaiaTV.com).

I believe a solar flash would cause all three to happen.

It is also envisioned as dividing into four quarters.

We can divide the 25,920-year cycle into four great years: In
north, south, east and west, spring, summer, fall and winter.
Buddha prophesized about a Messenger figure who arrives at
the end of an age in a cycle change, at the end of a Kappa,
known as the Maitreya. The Maitreya is derived from the
Sanskrit word maitri (lovingkindness), which is in turn derived
from the noun mitra, or (friend).

This seems very reminiscent of the Christian and Muslim
prophecies. The Maitreya says we will be free from all misery
and be able to cross the ocean of becoming. (Wilcock, *Wisdom
Teachings*, Nov.20, 2017 S27 Ep.15 www.GaiaTV.com).

This message, as you can see, is consistent throughout the
ages of ancient writings. It's the same message over and over
again. How we have forgotten all of this is a wonder. Religions

have taken these words, in some cases, and used them to trap us with into fear of what is to come. But I see this as a revelation to just be kind and loving toward each other, to treat others the way we would want to be treated. It seems so simple; we should clean up our own faults, be conscious of your own short comings, and try to live without fear.

In reviewing our past lives, we can see exactly what we have to work on. This helps us in moving forward. It's not the only way, but it's astounding to learn why we think and feel the way we do. Why certain fears and phobias that can and should be resolved carry overs from earlier lives.

THE END OF THE STRUGGLE

As a young girl, I used to sit for hours on end wondering what this life was all about. "If I was supposed to die in the hospital at the age of three, then why am I still here?" I wondered. "Why did I have to go through all of that drama just to end up questioning the point of it all?" And subsequently, being raised in a dysfunctional family imbued with domestic violence, living in fear day in and day out, waiting on pins and needles for the next shoe to drop, expecting to be attacked by the monster – my dad. My dad was so unpredictable. He suffered with borderline personality disorder, and I never knew what would set him off next. I used to have the same nightmare again and again about running and hiding, praying that the bad guys wouldn't find me. I'd wake up in a sweat, paralyzed with fear. For what? What was the end game?

The regression of the Midwest girl, who ran from the Native American only to be found and scalped, was the same story I was living: running and hiding from my dad, hoping and praying he wouldn't find me. Trying to be invisible so I wouldn't provoke him into yet another tirade. The realization that the Native American in that life was my dad in this life was almost too much to bear. No wonder I was so terrified of him. I thought he was going to kill me again. He terrorized all of us. I couldn't wait to grow up so I could get out of that house and be on my own.

Things did improve when I was finally able to move out of my parents' house and live on my own. But it was never easy.

That nagging question still remained. Does it always have to be this difficult? Working in a residential treatment center I found out that many children suffered far worse than I had up to that point in my life. I wouldn't have wanted to trade places with any of them. Again, I had to ask, "What's the point of all this? Why do these seemingly innocent children have to suffer?" It wasn't until I started to dig into past life regression therapy that I got some answers.

I understood that we can't keep running away from our fears. We must face them head-on. I devised a little guided imagery journey to find out exactly what each person's fear was. I theorized that if we can overcome our fears, then our struggles will be greatly diminished. It's our fear that keeps us shut down. The guided imagery tape was designed to help my client relax into a meditative state, because one can't be anxious and relaxed at the same time. This is called systematic desensitization, a theory developed by Wolpe, (1969). Wolpe held the notion that what we fear in reality is paralleled in the imagination; thus, that which we no longer fear in the imagination will not disturb us in reality. In order for the complex to come up, the defense mechanism must be quieted down. The name of the guided imagery journey is "Meet the Dragon." This guided imagery is available on my web site www.pastliferegressionny.com

Of course, I experimented on myself first, in my initial journey to meet the dragon, I hid. Of course, I did, that was my modus operandi. It didn't surprise me at all. I just stayed out of the way until the dragon went back into his cave and I could sneak away to safety. That doesn't solve the problem of confronting one's greatest fear. What I did was avoid a confrontation which accomplishes nothing.

One young man I worked with was about sixteen years old and a prominent gang member from the streets of New York City. I had been working with him for about a year when I decided this guided imagery might be just the thing to get him to open up. He had developed quite an extensive defense mechanism that he kept tightly in place. I had made some inroads with art therapy, but I needed to go deeper to find out what made him tick. He agreed to listen to my tape, and to be honest, I was genuinely shocked by the result.

In the journey, he traveled up the mountain to the dragon's cave. The dragon came out, saw the boy, and breathed fire on him. He was killed in an instant. I was stunned. "He was one of the most notorious gang members," I thought. "Surely he would put up a fight." But, no, he was totally defenseless against the dragon. That was when I realized why he was in the gang. He needed it to survive. He didn't think he could make it out there on his own. He wasn't so tough after all; under all that bravado, he was just a scared little boy who needed to be loved and protected. Of course, he would never let me know that, but after that session, our work together changed dramatically. He was finally able to progress in a way that met his needs, and the healing began.

Another boy I worked with did the same exercise. I wrote about him in my first book, but it's worth mentioning again here. He journeyed up the mountain to the dragon's cave, and when he arrived, he found the dragon asleep. "Okay, great," I thought. "He doesn't have to confront the dragon, and he'll be safe." But I was wrong. He went into the cave and woke the dragon up by throwing a rock at his head and hitting him in the eye. The huge dragon awoke but began whimpering as if he had been injured. The boy felt sorry for the dragon and rushed to his aid, offering to help clean the wound and dress it with salve. The dragon was so appreciative that he told the boy how lonely he was and asked him to stay. The boy decided to stay with the dragon, and they became friends. The dragon asked the boy what he could do for him in return, and the boy asked to be taken home. The dragon obliged the boy and allowed him to climb on top of his head. The two took off and flew all the way back to the boy's home.

The metaphor for this journey is that the boy was put into residential treatment because his parents were divorced and his father, who had custody, wasn't taking care of him. The boy wondered off and got into trouble because there was no supervision at home. He needed to get his father's attention. By hitting the dragon (his father) in the eye, the boy woke his father up to his needs. Then his father was able to take him home. After the journeywork we did, the boy realized it was up to him to wake his dad up and tell him what he needed. His dad finally got the message and was able to get his act together by taking parenting classes. Within six months of journeying to meet the dragon, the boy was released from the residential center and back into the custody of his dad.

There is one more dragon story I want to share with you. Another boy agreed to take the journey and found the mountain. He climbed to the top and went into the cave, where he saw cave drawings. He found a lit torch and followed the channel through the cave to a hidden passageway. He heard chanting from deep inside the cave. In a chamber, he found a group of elders. These wise men recognized the boy. They told him they had been waiting for him, and that he would be given all the gifts he needed to grow into a strong young man. They gave him a book to honor his great intelligence, a shield to protect him from the things he didn't need, and discernment to know what was good for him and what wasn't, especially who he could trust and who he should stay away from. And finally, they gave him a bow and arrow so he would be armed for battle and able to protect himself. They all congratulated him and told him he was now ready to go out into the world.

He left the cave only to find the dragon waiting outside for him. He fought the dragon but didn't kill him. He didn't have to. He made it known that he could fight the dragon and beat him, but that he had compassion for the dragon and wasn't afraid of him. He would rather let him be because he knew he might need his services later. In the end, the boy and the dragon had mutual respect for each other. This boy was smart enough to know never to burn his bridges, but to be firm and stand his ground. I never worried about him again after this journey because I knew he had everything he needed to be successful in his life.

You see, we all have to combat our demons in our own way. The first time I went to find the dragon, I hid from him. I needed to go find him again after all the work I had done, to see where I stood with him now. I had to literally go in search of the dragon. My travels took me to Ireland, where fairies and dragons are alive and well. Of course, they don't live in the open; one has to go and find them in the fifth dimension. I was called to Beltany circle, near Donegal, Ireland. This is the site of a five-thousand-year-old stone circle from the Celtic era, when fairies and dragons still roamed the earth, before they were driven into hiding. We have forgotten all of this because a blanket of sleep has covered mankind. We have lost our connection to the sacred earth and all of its magic, which was once commonplace. You see, the dragons are the keepers of the knowledge of the planet, and the fairies are the original light-beings who brought this planet into existence. They are the bridge to other dimensions, and according to folklore, they are waiting to come back when we learn to live in harmony with the planet once again.

At Beltany, I was able to dream and connect with the spirit of the place. The message I got from the stones was that when the earth quakes, the dragons will once again awaken and return to the surface. I was being called down under the stones to a cavern deep inside the earth. There, I met Merlin, and he was able to show me the way to where the dragon lay. She was sleeping, as the earth hadn't shaken her awake yet, but I was amazed at her size. She was immense, and I was able to touch her and massage her leathery skin. I walked around her, taking in her majesty. All of a sudden, I heard a little cry. When I looked further, I found a tiny baby dragon curled under its mother. He was awake, full of energy, wanting to come out and play with me. He wagged his tail and licked my face as if we were old friends. Merlin told me the baby would grow up to be a very powerful magical being and that he wanted to become my friend as a way of connecting to humans and helping them birth a new and wondrous age. I was flattered as I took it all in. I stayed there with the baby dragon for a while, we played and played but then it was time for me to go. I told him I would return when the time was right to resume our connection. What a wonderful dream.

The metaphor for this dream is renewal, rebirth of what is magical, the hope of a new earth that is alive and vibrant, healthy and beautiful in all her splendor. That is a far cry from running and hiding from the dragon. There is no need to struggle when you can dream a dream like this one. The earth is full of wonder; we have just forgotten how to listen to her. The Native American and aboriginal people have never forgotten how to listen to the earth mother. If we respect her, she will give us everything we need. When we free ourselves from guilt, shame, fear, hopelessness, and helplessness, there is nothing that can hold us back. Face your greatest fear, and you will be like a child full of wonder and joy.

"The most beautiful things in the world cannot be seen or touched, they are felt with the heart."
– Antoine de Saint-Exupéry, *The Little Prince*

Fig. 17, The Dragons by G. C. De Pietro

BIBLIOGRAPHY

Holy Bible. (King James Version)
https://www.biblestudytools.com

www.biblestudytools.com/kjv/matthew/
passage/?q=matthew+13:24-30

Ibid., Matthew 13:31-41(KJV)

Ibid., Matthew 13:42-44(KJV)

https://www.biblestudytools.com/kjv/2-peter/passage/?q=2-
peter+3:13-14

https://www.biblestudytools.com/kjv/isaiah/65-17.html

Ibid., Isaiah 66:22 (KJV)

https://www.biblestudytools.com/kjv/luke/
passage/?q=luke+21:25-28

*The Book of Enoch: The Apocrypha and Pseudepigraphia of the Old
Testament.* H.R. Charles Oxford: The Clarendon Press. www.
ccel.org/c/charles/otpseudepig/enoch/ENOCH_1.HTM.

Book of Enoch 1:3

Book of Enoch 45:3

Elkins, Don, Rueckert, Carla, and McCarty, James Allen,
The Ra Material: The Law of One, (Atglen, PA: Whitford Press,
1984).

Freud, Sigmund (1989) *The Ego and the Id*, W.W. Norton & Company, New York, NY

Image of Euston Station London, England.

https://s3-eu-west-1.amazonaws.com/smgco-images/images/54/590/medium_1945_0052_0001.jpg

Image of Emperor Wu. https://upload.wikimedia.org/wikipedia/commons/thumb/0/0d/Jin_Wu_Di.jpg/220px-Jin_Wu_Di.jpg

Jung, C. G. (1970) *Psychology Reflection*, Princeton, N.J., p. 220.

Law of One Session 14 Question 14–15 p.138

Ibid., Session 6 Question 13 pp. 92,93

Ibid., Session 14 Question 15 p. 138

Kalupahana, J. David, *The Buddhist Prophecies: The Buddhist Conception of Time and Temporality. Time and Temporality,* University of Hawaii Press 24, (2), 1974, 181–191.

Heartsong, Claire, *Anna, Grandmother of Jesus.* London: Hay House, 2002.

Hixon, Lex. *The Heart of the Qur'an: An Introduction to Islamic Spirituality,* 2nd ed. Wheaton, Il; Quest Books, 2003.

Meditation on the Holy Qur'an p.71

Ibid., Qur'an 77:8,15

Ibid., Qur'an 76:6-13

Ibid., Qur'an 88:1-5

Ibid., Qur'an 82: 10-12

Ibid., Qur'an 99: 4

Ibid., Qur'an 42:7

Ibid., Qur'an 5:51

Myss, Caroline, *Sacred Contracts*. New York: Three Rivers Press, 2002.

Tyrolean Couple, google images.com https://i.pinimg.com/236x/67/a1/c5/67a1c5fd16c7d4d6029570ac0ebbd9b9--folk-costume-austria.jpg

https://www.pinterest.com/pin/480407485224129972/

Stemman, Roy. *The Big Book of Reincarnation*. San Antonio, TX: Hierophant Corp., 2015.

Tick, Edward. *War and the Soul*. Wheaten, IL: Quest Books, 2005.

Wilcock, David. *The Ascension Mysteries*. New York: Penguin Group, 2016.

Wilcock, *Wisdom Teachings*, March,2014 S8 Ep.1 www.GaiaTV.com).

Wilcock, *Wisdom Teachings*, March,2016 S20 Ep.5 www.GaiaTV.com).

Wilcock, *Wisdom Teachings*, Sept. 25, 2017 S27 Ep.7 www.GaiaTV.com).

Wilcock, *Wisdom Teachings*, Nov.6, 2017 S27 Ep.13 www.GaiaTV.com).

Wilcock, *Wisdom Teachings*, Nov.13, 2017 S27 Ep.14 www.GaiaTV.com).

Wilcock, *Wisdom Teachings*, Nov. 20, 2017 S27 Ep.15 www.GaiaTV.com).

Wolpe, Joseph. *Psychotherapy by Reciprocal Inhibition*. Stanford, CA: Stanford University Press, 1958.

Woodcuts from History of Medieval Torture Devices.

https://www.pinterest.com/
pin/379287599858520073https://www.google.com-
arch?q=woodcuts+of+History+of+Torture&hl=en&tbm=is
ch&tbs=rimg:Cawde5ru64UDIjiLejX6wprceQ0AabjPXQ7
RcexhKw4ME82oHxOdEF4rcrZlKvNxUqce2gdoc2RPXY-
QI1B9MWOCf6yoSCYt6NfrCmtx5EXNr6mN43cxnKhI-
JDQBpuM9dDtER1MW0czg-GjEqEglx7GErDgwTzREjUf
yUVsDg3ioSCagfE50QXityEfumVcb_1ETOtKhIJtmUq83FS
px4RV9zgLzDLUqcqEgnaB2hzZE9dhBFV5k5iBgIn8yoSCQ
jUH0xY4J_1rEWE-sHZhWLWy&tbo=u&sa=X&ved=2ahU
KEwj_iOLuip7jAhUQh-AKHdsMAl0Q9C96BAgBEBs&biw
=1034&bih=589&dpr=1#imgdii=u6VICVSNKLiOmM:&i
mgrc=Cg5v8Jt17QMSiM:

Woolger, Roger. *Other Lives, Other Selves*. London: Bantam
Books, 1988.

Courtesy of Emily Trapp, Photographer

ABOUT THE AUTHOR

Ms. De Pietro is an artist, regression therapist, and writer. She lives in the Hudson Valley with her husband Jack and does regression work in her office and on Skype.

Skype address: gloria.depietro24

For information about workshops or MP3s of the guided imagery tapes used in this book, visit

www.pastliferegressionny.com